Artist: Francine Auger

John Franklin, 1786-1847.

John Wilson

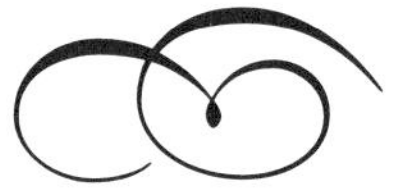

Trained as a geologist, John Wilson is now a full-time writer. After an Honours degree from St. Andrews University in Scotland and fifteen years as a research geologist, he began freelance writing in 1989. He has published five young adult novels. His first novel for children, *Weet*, a fantasy of time travel and dinosaurs, was published in 1995 (Napoleon). With the addition of *Weet's Quest* (Napoleon, 1997), and *Weet Alone* (Napoleon, 1999), it has grown into a trilogy. Drawing on a long-standing interest in history, Wilson wrote *Across Frozen Seas* (Beach Holme, 1997), a story set during the tragic Franklin Expedition of 1845. This theme expanded into an adult work, *North With Franklin: The Lost Journals of James Fitzjames* (Fitzhenry & Whiteside, 1999), a fictionalized journal of one of Franklin's officers. He returned to historical fiction for young adults with a book set during the Spanish Civil War (*Lost in Spain*, Fitzhenry & Whiteside, 2000). Wilson has also written a biography of Norman Bethune (*Norman Bethune: A Life of Passionate Conviction*, XYZ Publishing, 1999), Book 1 in The Quest Library collection.

Wilson teaches courses at Malaspina-University College in Nanaimo, and he tours to schools and conferences giving readings and workshops. He also writes reviews of both adult and children's books for *The Globe and Mail* and *Quill & Quire*. John Wilson lives with his family in Lantzville, British Columbia. Comments on his books may be sent to John at johnwilson-author@home.com

The Quest Library
is edited by
Rhonda Bailey

Editorial correspondence:
Rhonda Bailey, Editorial Director
XYZ Publishing
P.O. Box 250
Lantzville BC
V0R 2H0
E-mail: xyzed@telus.net

In the same collection

Ven Begamudré, *Isaac Brock: Larger Than Life.*
Lynne Bowen, *Robert Dunsmuir: Laird of the Mines.*
Kate Braid, *Emily Carr: Rebel Artist.*
William Chalmers, *George Mercer Dawson: Geologist, Scientist, Explorer.*
Stephen Eaton Hume, *Frederick Banting: Hero, Healer, Artist.*
Betty Keller, *Pauline Johnson: First Aboriginal Voice of Canada.*
Dave Margoshes, *Tommy Douglas: Building the New Society.*
Raymond Plante, *Jacques Plante: Behind the Mask.*
Arthur Slade, *John Diefenbaker: An Appointment With Destiny.*
John Wilson, *Norman Bethune: A Life of Passionate Conviction.*
Rachel Wyatt, *Agnes Macphail: Champion of the Underdog.*

John Franklin

Canadian Cataloguing in Publication Data

Wilson, John, 1951-

John Franklin : traveller on undiscovered seas

(The Quest Library ; 10).
Includes bibliographical references and index.

ISBN 0-9688166-1-4

1. Franklin, John, Sir, 1786-1847. 2. Canada, Northern – Discovery and exploration. 3. Explorers – Great Britain – Biography. I. Title. II. Series : Quest library ; 10.

FC3961.1.F73W54 2001 917.1904'1'092 C2001-940384-4
F1090.5W54 2001

Legal Deposit: Second quarter 2001
National Library of Canada
Bibliothèque nationale du Québec

XYZ Publishing acknowledges the support of The Quest Library project by the Canadian Studies Program and the Book Publishing Industry Development Program (BPIDP) of the Department of Canadian Heritage. The opinions expressed do not necessarily reflect the views of the Government of Canada.

The publishers further acknowledge the financial support our publishing program receives from The Canada Council for the Arts, the ministère de la Culture et des Communications du Québec, and the Société de développement des entreprises culturelles.

Chronology and Index: Lynne Bowen
Layout: Édiscript enr.
Cover design: Zirval Design
Cover illustration: Francine Auger
Photo researcher: Marilyn Mattenley
John Franklin's signature: National Archives of Canada, Reel A-1026

Printed and bound in Canada

XYZ Publishing
1781 Saint Hubert Street
Montreal, Quebec H2L 3Z1
Tel: (514) 525-2170
Fax: (514) 525-7537
E-mail: xyzed@mlink.net
Web site: www.xyzedit.com

Distributed by:
General Distribution Services
325 Humber College Boulevard
Toronto, Ontario M9W 7C3
Tel: (416) 213-1919
Fax: (416) 213-1917
E-mail: cservice@genpub.com

John FRANKLIN

TRAVELLER ON UNDISCOVERED SEAS

For my father

No; there are no more sunny continents – no more islands of the blessed – hidden under the far horizon, tempting the dreamer over the undiscovered sea; nothing but those weird and tragic shores, whose cliffs of everlasting ice and mainlands of frozen snow, which have never produced anything to us but a late and sad discovery of depths of human heroism, patience, and bravery, such as imagination could scarcely dream of.

Blackwood's Edinburgh Magazine,
November, 1855.
(Quoted in *Frozen in Time*
by Owen Beattie and John Geiger).

Contents

National Archives of Canada, C-028847

Trying to stay alive. Gathering *Tripe de Roche* for supper
at an encampment in the Barren Lands, 1821.

Prologue

At Fort Enterprise

"That's the man who ate his boots!"

Lieutenant John Franklin is sitting like a pathetic Buddha on the bare wooden boards of an almost-empty room in a makeshift fort thousands of miles from his home. Around him the wind howls unimpeded over a frozen eternity of ice and snow, a barren emptiness that uncaringly kills those who challenge it unprepared. The journey here has been long, but it is almost over. The days are darkening into winter, a winter Franklin cannot survive. Life has apparently fled this harsh landscape - fled to the south where there is food and warmth, or into hibernation where neither is necessary. Franklin cannot flee, he is too weak, and if he sinks into hibernation he will never arise from it.

Perhaps he is dreaming of the friendly fields of his English home and regretting he did not follow his father's footsteps to become a comfortable provincial businessman. More likely he is dreaming of food, for John Franklin is starving to death. His skin is pale beneath the dirt that has not been washed off for weeks. His clothes are filthy and in tatters and they hang from his skeletal frame as if made for a much larger man. Franklin is only occasionally in touch with reality and is so weak he cannot stand without assistance. His eyes drift in and out of focus as they wander around the room. In the corner lie the bodies of two men. They have been dead for several days and are beginning to smell, but no one living has the strength to drag the dead outside. Beside Franklin lies a third man. He is not dead yet, but it is hard to tell by looking at him. His breathing is so shallow as to be undetectable, and the only signs of life are the occasional grunts that he emits in response to whatever fevered dream is passing through his brain. It will be only a matter of hours before he joins the two in the corner.

Although he looks closer to sixty, John Franklin is only thirty-five. It is November 7, 1821, and this is the culmination of Franklin's first great expedition. Three-and-a-half months before, Franklin, with midshipmen Robert Hood and George Back, doctor and naturalist John Richardson, able seaman John Hepburn, and fifteen voyageurs and hunters, had set off into the unknown from the mouth of the Coppermine River on Canada's Arctic coast. Since then, they have mapped 1030 kilometres of previously unexplored coastline, but at a terrible cost. Hood has been murdered and Back is missing. One man has been executed, and nine others lie dead of starvation, their bodies scattered in the snow across the Barren Lands. Now the survivors are back where they began, at Fort Enterprise. Perhaps someone will find their records and their frozen bodies next spring.

Richardson and Hepburn are with Franklin. They have managed to drag themselves outside to collect some wood. They do not have the strength to both gather wood for the fire and collect food. It is bitterly cold. The fire takes priority. At least they will die warm.

The wood collecting is painfully slow work. It is nearly impossible for the men to make their starved bodies do what they want. Their joints ache, their limbs are swollen, their gums are bleeding, and their teeth are getting loose. Their skin is covered with sores, and they are beginning to lose touch with reality. Visions of impossible banquet tables laden and groaning with rich foods float before them. They have even begun to steal hungry glances at the bodies of their dead companions. For weeks their meals have consisted of soup made from pounded, putrid deer bones, fried or boiled animal skins, and *Tripe de Roche*, a lichen scraped off the rocks around them. The skins and bones had been discarded the previous spring and were buried in lime ash, which makes the soup from boiling them so alkaline that it rips the skin from the explorers' mouths and throats when they drink it. Without enough to sustain them, their bodies are consuming themselves.

Richardson and Hepburn spend the entire day working and have only enough wood for one fire.

Hepburn is bending over to pick up a piece of kindling when a faint noise penetrates his befuddled brain. Agonizingly slowly he stands up. Richardson has heard it as well. The two men look at each other, hardly daring to believe what it might mean. There it is again. This time there can be no doubt – it is a musket shot.

George Back has not died in the wilderness. He has completed an epic journey, found a First Nations band only two days previously, and sent three of them back to the fort with a supply of fresh meat.

Richardson and Hepburn, staggering with weakness and excitement, scramble back to tell Franklin – food is on the way. They are saved in the nick of time. Ironically, the very food that saves their lives almost kills them. Unable to stop, they gorge on the rich meat the hunters bring and lie for days in agony. But they do revive, although it is the spring of the next year before they fully recover their strength.

By October 1822, Franklin is back in London, where he is considered a hero. His saga of starvation, murder, and cannibalism captures the public imagination. He is recognized on the street, promoted to Captain, and made a member of the Royal Society. His 180,000-word *Narrative of a Journey to the Shores of the Polar Sea in the Years 1819, 20, 21, and 22*, sells briskly. In quick succession, he marries, fathers a child, and discovers that his new wife is ill with consumption.

Given the horrors he has undergone in 1821, the gratifying recognition he receives upon his return, and his initiation into family life, one would not expect Franklin to rush immediately off into the wilds once more. One experience of severe starvation is usually enough. Yet, in February of 1825, leaving his baby daughter and dying wife behind, Franklin once more sets sail for the "shores of the polar sea."

Why did Franklin jump at every opportunity to risk his life? What pulled him back to the Canadian Arctic, not once but twice, and the second time to his death?

Of the forty-seven years from the time he joined the navy at age fourteen until he died at age sixty-one, John Franklin spent a bare dozen years at home in England. He was a restless man, a traveller who was never content to stay in one place in comfort and security. This characteristic led him to accomplish much, made his name a household word, and, eventually, killed him.

Even after his death, Franklin's life continues to fascinate writers. He has been presented as a hero, an honourable officer striving nobly against impossible odds. He has also been depicted as a fool, who doomed himself and his expedition through his inflexible, archaic attitude. More than 150 years after his men buried him in an unknown grave in the centre of the land that kept calling him back, there is no agreement on Sir John Franklin. Perhaps the restless traveller will never be laid to rest, the mystery never solved. Perhaps John Franklin's journey will never end.

National Maritime Museum, London, BHC0529. Artist: Nicholas Pocock.

John Franklin's first adventure. The Battle of Copenhagen, 1801.

1

Spilsby to Copenhagen

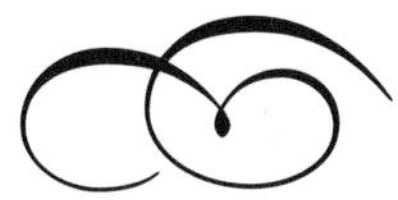

"When I arrived on the maindeck...there was not a single man standing the whole way from the mainmast forward,...I hastened down the fore ladder to the lower deck and felt really relieved to find someone alive."

Midshipman on HMS *Monarch*
at the Battle of Copenhagen

John Franklin grew up in Spilsby in Lincolnshire, the descendant of a long line of country gentlemen. His father, Willingham, was not an adventurous man, quite happy to spend his life as a respectable Spilsby merchant. Willingham married a farmer's daughter, Hanah Weekes, and most of the excitement in his life stemmed from helping to raise the couple's twelve children. John was number nine, the youngest of five boys.

One boy died in infancy, but as the others grew, it became clear to Willingham that none of the children would follow him into business. The wars against Napoleon and the expanding British Empire offered young men amazing opportunities to seek glory, wealth, and adventure in the far-flung corners of the globe. Despite the dangers of an early death from disease or violence, a merchant's life in Spilsby paled in comparison.

The oldest Franklin boy, Thomas Adam, went off to raise a regiment of volunteer cavalry and became its colonel. In 1807, after a disastrous financial speculation in which he lost all his own and much of his father's money, Thomas committed suicide at the age of thirty-three. Willingham's namesake attended Oxford, became a lawyer, went to India, was knighted, and became a Supreme Court Judge in Madras. He died of cholera in 1824 when he was forty-five. James, who was only three years older than John, joined the Indian army and served with distinction in the Pindari War. He was also a surveyor, mapmaker, and author of a geology text. James lived to be fifty-one. All these were common – and with the exception of Thomas's final disgrace, respectable – occupations for the young sons of the middle class in the late eighteenth and early nineteenth centuries, and they influenced John.

Franklin was also very close to his seven sisters, and it was from them that he derived the gentleness that marked his life. The letters where he discusses personal matters are all addressed to his sisters, not to his parents or brothers. He wrote to them all, but his favourite was Isabella. She married Thomas Cracroft, and their daughter, Sophia, was to be an element in Franklin's later life.

At ten, young John was sent to board at Louth Grammar School, twenty-four kilometres north of Spilsby. The school was typical of the educational institutes of its day. Students were given a basic classical education. Learning to read the Greek and Roman poets in their original languages and practising discipline, teamwork, and proficiency at sports were the highest goals of education – much more important than studying science and mathematics. The author Thomas de Quincy called schools like Louth, "the peculiar glory of England," credited them with developing "superior manliness, generosity, and self-control," and claimed they got rid of "meanness, pusillanimity, or indirectness."

Certainly, Franklin aspired to manliness, generosity, and self-control, but whether he got these qualities from his time at Louth is unknown. In contrast to de Quincey's glowing testimonial, the poet Alfred Tennyson, who attended Louth early in the 1800s, said, "How I did hate that school! The only good thing I ever got from it was the memory…of an old wall covered with wild weeds opposite the school windows." Whatever John Franklin thought of Louth, it was from there that he set out on his life's journey.

When he was eleven years old, Franklin and some school friends travelled the fourteen kilometres from Louth to the village of Saltfleet on the coast. It was the first time John had seen the sea, and the effect was electrifying. The vastness of the dark, rolling North Sea, the mystery of what lay over the flat horizon, and the apparent confidence with which the white-sailed British men-of-war tacked up and down the coast exerted a pull on Franklin that he was never to overcome.

Watching his older brothers go out into the world and struggle, successfully or not, to better their social position and expand their horizons, had taught John that he did not want to settle down in his father's grocery shop. Nor, despite being a pious young man, did he want to fulfill Willingham senior's wish that he enter the clergy, but it wasn't until he saw the sea that he knew which direction he would go.

At the first school holidays, Franklin rushed home and enthusiastically informed his father that he was going to be a sailor.

"I would rather follow you to the grave than the sea," a horrified Willingham responded.

But John perservered. In his mind he pictured "both the hardships and pleasures of a sailor's life" and was so certain that it was the life for him that no other course was possible. And there was a family connection to the sea that John could cite as precedent. An aunt had married the explorer Matthew Flinders.

Fortunately for the youngest Franklin boy, Willingham was not an unreasonable man. He realized that outright opposition to John would alienate him and cause a family rift, so he tried a more subtle approach. When John turned thirteen, he booked him passage on a merchantman sailing from Hull to Lisbon. Since the journey would traverse the Bay of Biscay, a stretch of water notorious for its storms and rough sea conditions, Willingham reasoned that this would cure his son of any romantic longings he harboured for the nautical life. The plan backfired. John returned even more determined than ever to become a sailor.

Showing remarkable wisdom and enlightenment for the times, Willingham bowed to the inevitable and obtained for John a position as first-class volunteer on HMS *Polyphemus*, a two-decked, sixty-four-gun man-of-war under the command of Captain Lawford. John Franklin joined his first ship on March 9, 1800, a month before his fourteenth birthday. A year later and only two weeks before his fifteenth birthday, Franklin's desire for adventure was fulfilled.

In early 1801, Britain's war against Napoleon was not going well. Austria had been defeated the year before, and Russia, Sweden, and Denmark had formed the League of Armed Neutrality to challenge Britain's right to intercept and search merchant ships bound for French ports. As a response, Britain sent a fleet of eighteen battleships to attack the Danish fleet at Copenhagen.

Sea battles in the days of wooden ships and before explosive shells were brutal affairs. It is very difficult to sink a wooden ship by punching holes in it with round shot. A lucky shot might set off an explosion or start a fire, but these rarely happened. More commonly, ships simply pounded away at each other for hours until they were little more than floating, mastless hulks filled with horribly mutilated bodies. The aim of attacking a ship became not to sink it but to kill so many of its crew that the survivors could not continue the fight, either because they were too few or because they had had enough and gave up.

When a solid round cannonball weighing fourteen kilograms went through a ship, it destroyed everything in its path. Ships' timbers and masts were shattered and wood splinters flew around like shrapnel. Human flesh did not even slow these projectiles down. In addition, when two ships were close enough, they fired grapeshot, clusters of small round shot designed to kill men on exposed decks, and chain shot, which had the dual purpose of destroying a ship's rigging and cutting in half any men in its way. Sharpshooters sat in the upper rigging and picked off sailors on the opposing ship's decks.

On the morning of Thursday, April 2, the British attack squadrons, under the command of Horatio Nelson, lay off Copenhagen harbour. The decks of the *Polyphemus* were scenes of tense activity. In the deepest levels of the ship the surgeons laid out their instruments in preparation for the gruesome work to come. Since they were below the waterline, they were relatively safe from the cannon shot, yet this was where the scenes of greatest horror occurred. Many of the surgeons and their assistants were barely trained butchers who could do nothing but hack off mutilated limbs and dig inexpertly for embedded musket balls and assorted pieces of wood and metal. The floor around them would soon be running with blood and the dark, cramped space echoing with the sound of the sailors' screams as the surgeons carried out their grisly tasks without the aid of anesthetics. If you were wounded, your chances of coming out of this hellish place were slim. No wonder some of the wounded refused to be taken below.

On the gun decks above the surgeons' heads, the gun ports were being swung up and secured. Each sweating, six-man gun crew laboured to roll their immensely heavy weapon out and make sure it was ready. Hawsers as thick as a man's arm were tied around the gun so that, when it fired, the recoil would not throw the tons of iron back across the deck to crush men and punch a hole in the ship's side. The powder monkey, a boy even younger and smaller than the teenage Franklin, stood nervously to one side with nothing to do until the battle began. Then his job would be one of the most dangerous. He would have to run through the ship to the powder magazine and fetch the charges for his gun. Carrying a bag of unstable explosives, he would have to negotiate wildly tilting decks, running, screaming sailors, cannonballs, and musket shot. If he failed, not only would there be very little left of him to find, but the resulting fire could put the entire ship in danger.

On the exposed upper decks, anything loose was stowed away. Marines with primed muskets took positions behind stacks of tightly rolled hammocks. On the quarterdeck, the officers strolled around, overseeing the activity and attempting to keep the tension under control by assuming an air of nonchalance. This was where young John Franklin stood, scared and wondering if life at sea was quite as attractive as he had imagined it. On the other hand, he was thrilled by the imposing spectacle of a battle fleet sailing to war, and he was excited by the adventure of it all.

At 10:30, the ships weighed anchor and sailed towards the Danish fleet. *Polyphemus* was second in line, and at 11:20, she and another ship, the *Isis*, anchored beside two Danish ships – one of seventy-four and the other of sixty-four guns – and commenced firing. As the ship's log briefly described it, "At noon a very heavy and constant fire was kept between us and the enemy, and this was continued without intermission until forty-five minutes past two, when the 74 abreast of us ceased firing.... We ceased firing and boarded both ships and took possession of them."

This clinical description gives no sense of the carnage wrought on board both the Danish and British vessels. *Polyphemus* got off lightly, having just six men killed and twenty-four wounded, although one of the dead was James Bell, a midshipman and a messmate of Franklin's. Other ships suffered much worse. In total the British lost 350 killed, and the Danes 6,000 killed, wounded, or prisoner.

Copenhagen is famous for Nelson's response to his Commander-in-Chief's flagged signal to break off the fight. When he was informed of the order, Nelson replied, "I have only one eye – I have a right to be blind sometimes." Then, putting his telescope to his blind eye, he turned towards the flagship and said, "I really do not see the signal!"

The story became part of Nelson's myth, but the battle turned out to have been unnecessary. On March 24, even before the battle was fought, the mad Czar

Paul of Russia was assassinated. Since he was the force behind the League of Armed Neutrality, it fell apart and would have done so without the bloodshed of April 2. Copenhagen was not the last pointless battle Franklin would fight in.

The Battle of Copenhagen made a strong impression on the sensitive boy of fourteen. Young Franklin, like other young people of his time, regarded war as glorious and battle as adventurous, but watching men being dismembered around him was an experience he never forgot. In later years he vividly recalled the sight of the large number of both British and Danish dead that he viewed through the clear water of Copenhagen harbour. Such an experience would have hardened some people, but in Franklin's case it left him with a desire to minimize suffering – an ironic consequence given the horrors which attended many of his later ventures.

National Library of Australia, S10659. Artist: Edward William Cooke.

A way station on a journey to the other side of the world.
A prison hulk at Portsmouth filled with convicts awaiting transport to Australia.

2

Around Australia

> "He is a very fine youth, and there is every possibility of his doing credit to the *Investigator* and himself. In a few months he will be sufficient of an astronomer to be my right-hand man in that way."
>
> Matthew Flinders on John Franklin

If, in 1801, you were caught stealing a loaf of bread, or poaching a pheasant or grouse from the land belonging to the local Lord, or if the government considered you to be a political risk, you had a good chance of ending up in Australia for the rest of your life. And the chances of that life being long were remote.

First you would be stored in a rotting hulk anchored on the Thames. You would live in the filthy, dark, damp hold, often with a six-kilogram iron ball chained to your ankle. Your spirit would be gradually broken by the degrading conditions, the harsh punishments, and the hopelessness of your situation. Eventually, there would be enough convicts on the hulks to warrant a transportation. These were contracted out to private firms, some of which had gained their experience transporting human cargoes on the slave ships across the Atlantic. If you were lucky, you got a good ship where only one in twenty or thirty died. If you were unlucky and the Captain was a brutal sadist, or was cutting back on space so he could carry cargo to sell, or if typhus broke out, one in three or four of your companions might die on the voyage. Arrival at the new colony of Port Jackson, soon to change its name to Sydney, brought little relief. There you would live until your sentence was up, little more than a working slave, subject to the whims of the officers in charge of the colony and a brutal punishment regime which included flogging until your back looked like hamburger.

Several thousand convicts, along with a similar number of free settlers, clung to the fertile strip of land around Port Jackson harbour. Inland, there was no room for expansion, it was just a wilderness of barren mountain ranges filled with bizarre animals and plants and unfriendly local inhabitants.

In your father's or your grandfather's day, you might have ended up in America, but the colonies there had revolted and were independent now. Port

Jackson was the only place remote enough for Britain to dump her unwanted populace, and that unwanted populace was growing. The British government was terrified of a revolution at home similar to the one the French had undergone in 1789. There was a lot of unrest. Early socialists were agitating for improved working conditions as the Industrial Revolution took hold of British society. Better, the government thought, to get rid of these troublemakers by sending them to Port Jackson. But Port Jackson was almost full, and there was no other obvious place where a convict colony could be started. More mapping of the poorly known Australian coast was needed. The job was given to Franklin's uncle, Matthew Flinders.

Before he sailed to fight at Copenhagen, Franklin was told that Flinders was ready to sail in his ship the *Investigator*. The young man was interested and thought he had a good chance of going with his uncle. The only problem was that he would be away when the *Investigator* sailed. Just in case he was back in time, Franklin wrote and asked his father to put in a good word for him with Flinders.

As it turned out, the Danish adventure was shorter than expected and Franklin returned to find his uncle still in England. He also found that his request to his parents had been answered and that Flinders was holding a space for him. His father had obviously resigned himself to his son's ambitions, but perhaps he felt that a voyage of exploration would be less dangerous than a battle. If he did, he was wrong.

Flinders was one of the best navigators of his age. He had been with Captain Bligh on his second voyage across the Pacific and he had experience of surveying the Australian coast. Flinders was the obvious man to lead the new venture. In July 1801 he set sail from England, with John Franklin as a newly promoted midshipman.

Flinders took Franklin under his wing and trained him in astronomy and navigation. It was a superb training for a young sailor with pretensions to exploration, and Franklin appreciated it. Flinders was happy with his young charge: "It is with great pleasure that I tell you of the good conduct of John.... His attention to his duty has gained him the esteem of the first lieutenant, who scarcely knows how to talk enough in his praise." Even given the family connection and Flinders' natural tendency to speak well of his nephew, Franklin was making a mark.

Franklin was a serious boy who took his new role to heart: "The first thing which demands attention is the learning perfectly my duty as an officer and seaman. It would be an unpardonable shame if after serving two years I was ignorant of it." He read Shakespeare, Junius, Smollett, a history of Scotland, and geographical and naval textbooks. He also regretted not spending more time on his French lessons since, when he met some French officers (England and France were enjoying a brief peace), they had to resort to his second language, Latin.

That Franklin did well with Flinders is proven in the large numbers of islands that Flinders named Franklin, Spilsby, or Louth. But all was not schoolboy fun. On a barren stretch of coast, one of the officers was speared four times by aggressive natives, and one evening in Sleaford Bay, the ship's master, Mr. Thistle; a midshipman, Mr. Taylor (a messmate of Franklin's); and six able seamen took the cutter and went ashore to look for fresh water. As darkness fell they began the return journey to the ships. They never arrived and no sign was ever found of the eight men. This incident was an odd little foreshadowing of Franklin's own final fate.

Flinders had known before they sailed that the *Investigator* was not in the best of condition. The navy had claimed the pressure of circumstances as a reason for not having something better available, and Flinders, keen to get going, had acquiesced. He did not realize how bad his ship was until she was beached for repairs after surveying the Gulf of Carpentaria on Australia's north coast. As the carpenters proceeded to repair the known leaks, they came upon previously unsuspected rotten timbers. They produced a report that was grim reading for men so far from home; if the *Investigator* met a strong gale, she would founder; if she ran aground, she would break up; in twelve months, not a sound timber would remain. Nothing could be done until they reached Port Jackson on the other side of the continent. Hoping for the best, they set off to complete the circumnavigation of the continent.

The voyage was a nightmare. Sailing the ship was tense work, for it leaked thirty-four centimetres of water an hour on some days, and the crew never knew when it would fall apart beneath them. Fresh food ran low and scurvy and dysentery took hold. Five men died before they arrived at Port Jackson and four more soon after. Franklin got his first glimpse of the downside of nineteenth-century exploration.

In Port Jackson, the *Investigator* was condemned as "not worth repairing in any country." With his mapping work incomplete, Flinders now had to return home to report on the *Investigator* and find a new ship to continue his explorations. He found passage on the *Porpoise* and chose Franklin to be among those who would accompany him. Since the journey required passage of the treacherous Torres Strait, two merchantmen, the *Cato* and the *Bridgewater*, asked to accompany the *Porpoise*, and the small convoy sailed on August 10, 1803.

On the night of August 17th, the warrant officer on lookout in the forecastle of the *Porpoise* called out that he could see breakers ahead. He was too late. The ship ground onto a previously unmapped coral reef and heeled over. The *Cato* followed shortly after. The *Bridgewater* was safe, but impossible to get to. The men on the *Porpoise* spent a worrying night constructing a makeshift raft in case their vessel broke apart. The crew of the *Cato* could do little except cling desperately to the forecastle of their ship as the waves pounded it to pieces beneath them. At daybreak, Flinders managed to rescue the men on the *Cato* before the ship broke up, although three sailors drowned in the attempt. Both crews and the supplies from the *Porpoise* were transferred to a nearby sandbar.

It should have been a matter of waiting only a few hours for rescue by the *Bridgewater*, but her commander, Captain Palmer, panicked and sailed off, deserting the shipwrecked crews. On arriving at Bombay, Palmer reported both the *Porpoise* and *Cato* lost with all hands. Ironically, on the next leg of its voyage home, the *Bridgewater* went down with Palmer and all her crew.

The ninety-four abandoned men were now stuck on an uncharted sandbar measuring about 274 by 46 metres, and only 1.5 metres above the sea. They had adequate supplies, including some live sheep and pigs, but no hope of rescue. Flinders realized it was important to keep his men busy. Sweating in the tropical sun, they dug a pit, raised one of the *Cato*'s masts, and placed a flag on top. It would serve the dual purpose of signalling any passing ship and laying national claim to the island.

Flinders also had his men lay out his charts of the Australian coast to dry. Unfortunately, something scared the sheep, and they stampeded across the carpet of paper. The sound of the sheep's hooves as they galloped over his invaluable papers must have horrified the explorer, but fortunately little damage was done. The charts survive to this day in the British Museum, complete with muddy hoofprints. The sheep were eaten.

The crew built tents and took inventory of their supplies. One insubordinate man was publicly flogged to reimpose discipline and Flinders' thoughts turned to the party's rescue. The only hope was a perilous small boat journey across 1207 kilometres of open ocean back to Port Jackson. On August 26, Flinders set off in the cutter, which he had renamed *Hope*. In only six weeks, he completed one of the great feats of nineteenth-century navigation and was back with help.

Franklin remained behind on the sandbar, but he was not idle. The men dug a saw-pit, set up a forge, and constructed a new ship from the timbers of the wrecked *Porpoise*.

After their rescue, the men of the shipwreck separated. Some had had enough of the sea and returned to Port Jackson to settle. Flinders continued his mapping on his way back to England. Oddly, Franklin didn't go with his uncle and instead took passage to China. This was a lucky decision because Flinders was captured by the French at Mauritius and held captive for six years. The experience was so hard that he lived for only three years after his release.

There were more adventures in store for Franklin. In January 1804, he was returning home from China as signal midshipman on the flagship of a small, heavily laden, lightly armed convoy of merchantmen under the command of Commodore Dance. One morning, a squadron of French warships appeared on the horizon. Slow and massively outgunned, the merchant ships were easy pickings for the French. But Dance was a man to be reckoned with. Instead of trying a futile escape, he decided on an extraordinary bluff. Ordering Franklin to raise his signal flags, Dance formed his ungainly fleet into a line of battle. As the French commander watched in disbelief, Dance attacked. With the merchantmen bearing down on them, the French reassessed their opponents. Surely, no one could be insane enough to attack heavily armed warships with merchant ships. This must be a trap of some sort. The French fleet turned tail and fled from its puny foe. To add insult to injury, Dance pursued the French for two hours before breaking off and resuming his voyage. Given the difference in the two fleet's strengths, it is probably just as well he didn't catch them. Franklin's luck was holding.

On returning to England in August, 1804, Franklin joined the *Bellerophon*. Coincidentally, as a young man ten years previously, Matthew Flinders had served on this ship.

Franklin was given six weeks leave before he joined his new ship. Although still only eighteen, Franklin had seen his fair share of adventure and hardship. He knew how abruptly life could end in those days and wrote in his first letter home: "I trust some kind person will not fail answering this by return and mention how every member of the family is – whether any of the Spilsby friends are dead,...and how my old acquaintances in and about Spilsby are. Some of them have, I expect, paid the debt of Nature."

Franklin's assumption that some of his young friends must have died in his three-year absence, especially since they were leading much safer lives than his, seems odd, but then, two hundred years ago, life was a much chancier proposition than it is now. Franklin's morbid preoccupation soon gave way to a cheerful dismissal of his own hardships. "Although mishaps seem to attend every companion of the voyage – viz., a rotten ship, being wrecked, the worthy commander being detained, and the great expense of twice fitting out – yet we do cheer ourselves with the well-founded idea that we have gained some knowledge and experience, both professional and general."

Six weeks was not much of a break for Franklin's family to reconnect with their much-changed son. His experiences had matured him, and in the quiet Lincolnshire evenings the seafaring young Franklin had many exciting tales to tell his father, who was preparing to retire from his staid life of commerce.

For Franklin the next year was a boring one spent blockading the French fleet at Brest. In the summer of 1805 the *Bellerophon* returned to England for supplies and then continued her blockading work at Cadiz and Cartagena, with only short breaks to escort convoys in the Mediterranean. While Franklin was doing this, his old commander from Copenhagen, Nelson, was chasing the French and Spanish fleets across the Atlantic and back as they attempted to concentrate in enough strength to escort an invasion force over the English Channel. At length the combined French and Spanish fleet settled into Cadiz. On October 19, 1805, Admiral Villeneuve, stung by Napoleon's lack of confidence in him, ordered his thirty-three warships out of Cadiz harbour. Just out of sight over the horizon, Admiral Nelson, midshipman Franklin, and the twenty-seven warships of the British fleet waited. Franklin's brief spell of boredom was about to end.

3

Cape Trafalgar to New Orleans

> "I was astonished at the coolness and undaunted bravery displayed by our gallant and veteran crew, when surrounded by five enemy's ships."
>
> Officer on *Bellerophon*

Daybreak on October 21, 1805. The sun rose in a clear blue sky and promised a fine day. The wind was light and the sea almost calm as the masts of the combined French and Spanish fleets appeared over the horizon like "a great wood on our lee bow." Majestically, the two fleets drew together. This was the last great naval engagement fought under sail and, unlike Copenhagen, it was fought in the open ocean.

National Maritime Museum, London, BHC0552. Artist: Denis Dighton.

A fate that Franklin escaped. Nelson shot down in his moment of triumph on the quarterdeck of HMS *Victory* at Trafalgar, 1805.

Many of the ships had been recently painted, the British in buff and black, the French in black and white, and the Spanish in the brighter red, white, and black. The white sails billowed out and the wooden spars were varnished and gleaming in the sunlight. The masts were rich with flags, multicoloured signal flags, the personal flags of the senior officers, and the huge national ensigns: the red and gold of Spain, the tricolour of France, and the Union Jack of Britain. Very few people ever got to see such a magnificent sight, and Franklin, with his love of the navy and things nautical, was impressed.

But he was also awed. Many of the combined fleet's ships were bigger, faster, and more heavily gunned than anything the British possessed. The biggest was the extraordinary Spanish flagship, *Santissima Trinidad*, considered by many to be the most beautiful ship afloat. With four gundecks, she towered over Nelson's *Victory* or Franklin's *Bellerophon*, and her 136 cannons had the potential to wreak terrible havoc amongst enemy sailors. However, the British had one advantage: they could fire their guns faster and more accurately than the enemy could. Thus they could kill more sailors and disable more ships, and, Nelson fervently hoped, win the coming battle. For all the beauty of the scene, there was brutal work to be done.

Nelson's novel strategy was to break the combined fleet's line. He hoped to do this by having two lines of his own sail at right angles to the enemy line. He led one line in the *Victory*, and his friend Collingwood led the other in the *Royal Sovereign*. The *Bellerophon* was sixth in Collingwood's line. Franklin's job that day was signals officer. He had to stand on the open deck with a telescope, read the flag signals from Nelson and Collingwood, and relay them to his own Captain Cooke. The last clear message he saw before the smoke of battle made his job difficult was Nelson's famous order, "England expects that every man will do his duty."

Everything was ready on *Bellerophon*, "Billy Ruffian" as she was affectionately known by her crew. Her sailors had cleared the decks and thrown sand down to aid the footing of the barefoot gunners and absorb the blood of the dead and wounded. Men wrapped scarves around their heads to protect their ears from the deafening noise of the cannon, and they drew up wills. Each man fortified his spirits with a half pint of rum. Everyone was scared, but few let it show. Some sailors danced a hornpipe. The gunners primed their cannons and chalked, "Bellerophon, Death or Glory" on the barrels.

The battle began as the first shots were fired at the *Royal Sovereign* around noon. Half an hour later, the *Bellerophon* broke through the enemy line, exchanging cannon shot with the *Bahama* and the *Montanes*. Hauling around, she closed with the French ship *L'Aigle*, and the rigging of the two became entangled. The battle raged between the two ships. The French tried to board but were driven off. The *Bellerophon* almost blew up when a grenade, thrown through one of the gun ports, exploded in the corridor outside the powder magazine. Fortunately, the explosion blew the magazine door closed and prevented destruction. French soldiers packed *L'Aigle*'s rigging and raked Bellerophon's open decks with musket shot. The *Bahama* returned to pour more cannon fire into the British ship. Others joined in, and at one point, the *Bellerophon*, with her main and mizzen masts gone, was fighting five enemy ships at once.

Through all this, Franklin was busy. He could not see any signals to relay, but one of his other duties was to make sure the main flag was kept flying. To lower it meant surrender. Twice the flag came down from enemy fire, and twice Franklin raised it.

The French musket fire made the open decks a deadly chaos. Captain Cooke died from a musket shot as he was reloading his pistols. One particular sniper in the French rigging was making life on the deck difficult. Franklin was talking with a friend, midshipman Simmons, when they saw a sailor wounded by the sniper. Simmons moved to help, but he had only gone a few steps when he shuddered, turned back to Franklin, and tried to speak. Then he collapsed on the deck, shot through the head. Franklin and a sergeant of Marines went to help the wounded sailor. As they carried him below, he was hit again and killed. "He'll have you next," Franklin told the sergeant. Grabbing a musket, the sergeant went below to try to get a sight on the sniper.

Franklin scanned the enemy rigging and spotted the sniper, who was aiming directly at him. He jumped behind the mast, and the musket ball intended for him embedded itself in the deck nearby. Franklin peered out to see the sniper fall from the rigging into the sea. The sergeant returned. "I killed him at the seventh shot," the man proclaimed proudly.

So badly damaged that they could barely continue to fight, the two ships drifted apart. *L'Aigle* was captured by another British ship and *Bellerophon* claimed the severely damage *El Monarca* as a prize.

The Battle of Trafalgar ended at almost six in the evening with a spectacular explosion like the one that had nearly happened earlier on *Bellerophon* when the grenade blew up near the powder magazine. Fire, burning down through the decks of the French ship *Achille*, reached its powder magazine. "In a moment," one observer wrote, "the hull burst into a cloud of smoke and fire. A column of vivid flame shot up to an enormous height in the atmosphere and terminated by expanding into an immense globe, representing, for a few seconds, a prodigious tree in flames, speckled with many dark spots, which the pieces of timber and bodies of men occasioned while they were suspended in the clouds."

The battle was over. The British fleet was severely damaged, but the French and Spanish were destroyed. Nelson's imaginative strategy had worked, but at a cost. Like Cooke on the *Bellerophon*, Nelson had been found by a sniper. A musket ball had entered his shoulder and lodged near his spine. He lived long enough to learn that the battle was won. His body was preserved in a cask of rum for the three-week journey back to England, where, amidst vast outpourings of national grief, he was buried in Westminster Abbey.

The *Bellerophon* lost her Captain, Master, and twenty-six crew dead. One hundred and twenty-seven men were wounded. Franklin was lucky. Out of the forty-seven men on the exposed quarterdeck, he was one of only seven neither killed nor wounded. In the official report of the battle, he was singled out for displaying "very conspicuous zeal and ability." However, there was a price to pay. The noise of battle left Franklin slightly deaf for the rest of his life.

Franklin took great pride in his navy experiences. Twenty years after Trafalgar, he saw the *Bellerophon*'s scarred battle flag preserved in a church in England. "You can well conceive the delight it afforded to me," he wrote, "especially as the preservation of it in the hour of battle was one of the particular parts of my duty as signals officer on that occasion."

John Franklin's involvement in the Battle of Trafalgar provides one of those strange coincidences that populate the darker corners of history books. Two threads of Canadian history crossed off the coast of Spain that day. One of the ships with which the *Bellerophon* exchanged fire was the *Bahama*. The captain of the *Bahama*, a rising star in the Spanish Navy, was less lucky than Franklin. After he disengaged *Bellerophon*, he was attacked by another ship, the *Colossus*. Before he could surrender his crippled ship, he was decapitated by a cannonball. That Spanish captain was Dionisio Alcala Galiano, who, with Malaspina, had mapped much of Canada's west coast in 1792 in his ship the *Sutil*. Among the few remaining Spanish names scattered through the Gulf Islands off Victoria, there is a Dionisio Point, Mount Sutil, and Galiano Island. It is slightly bizarre that two significant figures in Canadian exploration unknowingly, yet busily, tried to kill each other in one of the most famous naval battles of all time.

ꟹ

After Trafalgar, Franklin returned briefly to Britain while his ship was repaired. Then, like most of the rest of the fleet, the *Bellerophon* spent a year and a half cruising to make sure Britain's naval dominance remained and that her trade could be protected. In 1807, Franklin transferred to the *Bedford* as master's mate, but was soon promoted to acting lieutenant. His role as lieutenant was confirmed on February 11, 1808 as he sailed with the fleet to escort the deposed Portuguese royal family to Brazil.

Franklin did not like the Portuguese, and, in keeping with the outspoken nature of his times, had no qualms about saying so. He called them, "the most ungrateful inhabitants of the earth, for whom it is impossible to feel the slightest esteem or respect." With no apparent sense of irony, he went on to bemoan their "bigotry."

On one occasion at Madeira, Franklin went ashore to collect two deserters from the *Bedford* who were being held by a Portuguese sergeant. The serious, religious young Franklin was not impressed to find the sergeant drunk and using the prisoners as free labourers to thatch his own home. In order to take charge of the prisoners, Franklin had to argue long and hard with the increasingly belligerent man. The man uttered violent threats and, as Franklin euphemistically recalled later, expressed himself, "with such gestures as greatly to irritate my feelings." But Franklin could apparently keep his temper even under extreme provocation, and persistence paid off. He returned to the ship with the deserters, and the sergeant was left with holes in his thatch.

Franklin disliked Brazil too. He found it dirty, unhealthy, and overcrowded. This was a difficult time for Franklin. His father had made some poor financial decisions and his brother, Thomas Adam, was in the middle of his financial disaster. The family was in dire economic straits and the young Franklin could expect no money from home. For an ambitious officer trying to make good on his inadequate salary, this made life very difficult.

Things did not improve on Franklin's return to Britain in August, 1810. Just three months later, his mother died at the age of fifty-nine. There followed two years of tedious, depressing work blockading the remnants of the French fleet at Flushing and Texel. Despite the horrific carnage he had seen at Copenhagen and Trafalgar, Franklin was eager for the French to come out and fight. "Let us hope for the best and wait with patience," he wrote in a letter home. His patience ran out in 1812 and he applied for a transfer to see "the varieties of the service." His request was denied.

The years 1813 and 1814 provided some variety with cruises to the West Indies to escort merchant convoys. The second cruise supplied more variety than Franklin bargained for when the *Bedford* was ordered on to New Orleans, where a British force was gathering to attack the city.

By late 1814, the War of 1812 was drawing to its conclusion. The attack on New Orleans was the last futile act in this fruitless war. The attack was carried out because the British Army wished to deny the Americans the storehouse of the city and because the British Navy was hungry for glory and prize money. It was futile because, two weeks before the attack began, the participants had signed a peace treaty and word of this was on its way across the Atlantic. The two thousand British soldiers who were killed or wounded in the hopeless frontal assault on the city suffered for nothing.

The navy's role consisted of securing Lake Borgne for the British so that they could approach the city itself. In forty-five rowing boats, Franklin and 1000 others attacked the five American gunboats on the lake. After a brief but violent battle, the American boats were captured. But the British losses were disproportionately high, seventeen killed, and seventy-seven, including Franklin himself, wounded. Franklin was awarded a medal for his role in the attack and Mentioned in Dispatches. His wound could not have been that bad since he was soon back in action, supervising the digging of a canal to enable the troops to approach the city.

After the disastrous attack, the *Bedford* returned to Britain, where she arrived on May 30, 1815. If Franklin was still looking for adventures against the French, he was disappointed. In June, Wellington finally defeated Napoleon at Waterloo and the Napoleonic Wars ended. Franklin would have to seek adventure elsewhere.

4

Towards the North Pole

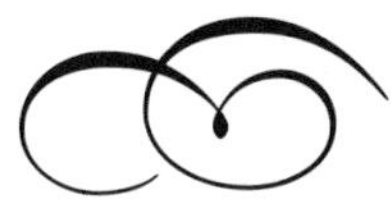

"The piece that had been disengaged at first wholly disappeared under water, and nothing was seen but a violent boiling of the sea and a shooting-up of clouds of spray.... After a short time, it raised its head full a hundred feet above the surface, with water pouring down from all parts of it, and then...after rocking about some minutes, it at length became settled."

Lieutenant Beechey
describing an iceberg calving.

With the end of the Napoleonic Wars, Britain was left with a surplus of ships and crews. Sailors were laid off, officers sent home on half pay, and ships

National Archives of Canada, C110045.

Two of the northern dangers Franklin encountered in 1818.
An iceberg and some walrus in Hudson Strait.

decommissioned. It was a waste of years of training, but there was one area where this surplus could be usefully employed – exploration.

In 1817, a well-respected whaling master, William Scoresby, returned from Baffin Bay to announce that the summer had been one of the most ice-free on record and that large areas of the Greenland coast, which were normally icebound all year, were open. The timing was perfect. Why not send idle ships and crews to discover something of this poorly understood corner of the globe?

The High Arctic was barely imaginable to the people of Franklin's time. It was their equivalent of the moon – incredibly remote and inhospitable – and the explorers who went there were the Apollo astronauts of their day. It took determination and the latest technology to get explorers into the Arctic and keep them alive. To go there was to live life on the edge – and a narrow, slippery edge it was.

There were two incentives to send expeditions to the far North. The first was the lure of the fabled Northwest Passage, the shortcut to the riches of the Orient. Drake, Frobisher, Hudson, and Cook had all searched for it and failed. By the early nineteenth century, enough stories had been told about the North to make most merchants realize that there was no commercial route through the ice, but the magic of the myth still pulled people on.

The second incentive was scientific research: natural history in general, but, more specifically, magnetism. Terrestrial magnetism was poorly understood, yet it was essential to navigation between the territories of

Britain's far-flung and growing empire. The navy needed to know about it. They also needed to know about the aurora borealis, which was thought to be electrical in nature and related to magnetism. A raging debate was underway in scientific circles on the nature of natural electricity and magnetism. Exploration close to the magnetic pole, where the aurora was strong, held out the promise of answering some very basic questions.

Even in the popular imagination, electricity and magnetism loomed large. They were considered fundamental forces with a limitless potential and imbued with almost supernatural powers. After all, hadn't it been these very forces which had animated the monster's dead tissue in Mary Shelley's immensely popular story, *Frankenstein*?

In 1818, Sir Joseph Banks, President of the Royal Society, and John Barrow, Second Secretary of the Admiralty, succeeded in persuading the government to mount two Arctic expeditions. The ambitious nature of both merely indicated how little people at that time knew about conditions in the Arctic.

One expedition was charged with sailing through the Northwest Passage from the Atlantic to the Pacific Oceans. The fact that some of the greatest explorers in history had failed abysmally to do this over the previous three hundred years did not discourage anyone. The second expedition was even more ambitious and unrealistic. It called for a ship to sail straight north, discover the North Pole, continue on through the Bering Strait, and eventually reach the Sandwich Islands (Hawaii).

The Northwest Passage venture was led by John Ross and had Edward Parry as second-in-command.

They mapped the west coast of Greenland and the east coast of Arctic Canada. Unfortunately, the expedition is mainly remembered for discovering a range of nonexistent mountains which Ross believed blocked Lancaster Sound. In reality, Lancaster Sound is the entrance to the Northwest Passage, a fact that Parry suspected despite his commander's opinions.

The Polar expedition was commanded by David Buchan, who had been the first European to make contact with the First Nations of Newfoundland. Second-in-command was Lieutenant John Franklin. Buchan commanded the whaler *Dorothea* with twelve officers and forty-three crew. Franklin's first command was the *Trent*, a smaller whaler with ten officers and twenty-eight crew.

Franklin's motives in becoming an explorer were not entirely a pursuit of adventure. One way for a half-pay officer to advance his career in the inactive years after 1815 was through exploration. When Franklin applied for the job of Buchan's second-in-command, he expressed concern that he might return with his health shattered after an expedition of perhaps five or six years. Patrons and friends with influence might have moved or died and all this would hurt his chances of promotion. Therefore he asked, "I should hope, were an offer ever made to me, it would be accompanied by a promotion."

An offer was made – without any guarantee of promotion. Despite that, Franklin jumped at the chance. The appeal of escaping the boredom of inactivity was too great.

The expeditions aroused considerable interest, and the number of visitors to the ships was so high that it hampered preparations. Many of the visitors were men of science, eager to discuss their pet theories of the unknown North with the ship's officers. Franklin was not much help. He thought it ridiculous that he had to talk to these experts considering "how little I know of the matters which usually form the subject of their conversations."

However, one visitor caught Franklin's attention. Eleanor Ann Porden was only nineteen, yet already she was quite outspoken for a young lady of that time. She had a keen interest in science, which explains her visit, and she had some pretensions to being a poet. Despite having little in common, the pair impressed each other.

Franklin's first venture into the Arctic began on April 25, 1818. Oddly, exactly thirty years later, this date would be significant to the survivors of Franklin's last visit to the North. Almost as soon as they set sail, the crews discovered that the quality of ships given to exploring parties had not improved since Flinders' voyage. The *Trent* had several leaks. The crew patched some of these at the Orkney Islands, but the worst one eluded detection, and so the pumps had to be manned every watch.

At Spitzbergen, north of Norway, the expedition found its way blocked by heavy ice. There they met some Russian hunters who were collecting walrus skins and tusks. The walrus were so numerous and so aggressive that they attacked and almost destroyed one of the *Trent*'s longboats during a hunting expedition.

The large beasts rushed the boat in a mass, hitting it with their tusks or butting it with their heads. Harpoons and axes merely slid off the animals' thick hides. It could have been a disaster, but one man managed to load his musket in the wildly swaying boat and fire it at the largest walrus, which appeared to be leading the attack. Immediately, the others stopped the assault and swam off, dragging the body of their leader with them.

As the expedition waited for the ice to break up, Franklin kept busy mapping and exploring the area. Numerous glaciers calved into Magdalena Bay where the ships were anchored. No one was really familiar with this phenomenon and they examined it closely. Unfortunately, they were also not familiar with the consequences of calving.

With Franklin in command, a group of men set out in a launch to examine the end of the bay. All at once, the men heard a report as loud as a cannon from above their heads. Looking up, Franklin watched in horror as a huge piece of ice, sixty-one metres above them, broke away from the face of the glacier and plunged down. The men frantically rowed to keep the boat pointed towards the immense wave they knew was coming, and watched as the iceberg crashed into the sea with a noise clearly heard on the *Dorothea*, six kilometres away.

As their small boat was thrown around like a cork by the wave, Franklin knew they would be lucky to survive. When things calmed down, they approached the iceberg and measured it: it was eighteen metres high, 400 metres around, and about 426,720 tonnes in weight.

Buchan attempted several times to lead his expedition north, but they were met each time by a vast impenetrable wall of ice. On one occasion, they were trapped for two weeks, on another, three weeks. While they were forced to remain idle, the crew of the *Trent* did manage to discover the leak that had so bothered them on the voyage north – it had been caused by a bolt which a shipyard worker had forgotten to install.

When open water appeared and leads seemed to offer a way through the ice, the two small vessels sailed in. Invariably, the leads closed and the ships became beset. Then the crews had to take to the ice, laboriously cut holes ahead of the ships, and physically pull them forward. It was gruelling work, and often the small distance they managed to drag the ships was cancelled out by the drift of the ice in the opposite direction when they were held fast.

On one occasion, the pressure of the ice was so great that it lifted the ships up and twisted the hulls. Men watched helplessly as doors flew open and the timbers cracked deafeningly around them. Another time, they were caught in a gale close to the coast of Spitzbergen. The wind was driving them onto the rocky coast and certain destruction. Buchan decided that their only hope lay in sailing directly into the loose pack ice, where huge blocks of ice were being thrown around by the wind and waves. It was terrifying, for these loose blocks of ice could easily stave in the sides of the ships. Franklin took what precautions he could. He ordered the men to hang cables and iron plates over the sides to protect the hull. He had everything movable tied down and the masts strengthened.

Even so, the shock of sailing into the ice almost broke the *Trent*'s masts. Ice floes twice the size of the ship ground against her hull with a rending noise. All around the tiny vessels, the ice and waves rose and fell in a terrifying scene. Through the overwhelming noise the crew could hear the continuous mournful tolling of the ship's bell.

After hours of this punishment, the gale abated and the expedition escaped to open water to assess the damage. Ice had so broken in the side of the *Dorothea* that her crew wondered how she had survived. Obviously she could not continue exploring. Franklin wanted to continue with the *Trent*, but the *Dorothea* was so badly damaged that it was doubtful she could even make it back to England, and so the *Trent* was forced to accompany her to render assistance if needed. Apparently, the open ice conditions that Scoresby had reported in 1817 had simply been a temporary condition. A very similar, variable weather pattern thirty years in the future would lure an overconfident Franklin and his ships to their doom.

The ships' carpenters did their best to repair the *Dorothea* and the *Trent* in preparation for the voyage home. The officers took magnetic observations and carefully surveyed the coast. On August 30, the expedition set sail and on October 22, 1818, arrived back in London.

Geographically, Buchan's Polar expedition achieved little; certainly it came nowhere close to the optimistic expectations. However, it gave Franklin his first taste of the Arctic and a glimpse of the violence and dangers of ice and climate in the northern lands.

The expedition also marked the opening of the golden age of British Arctic exploration. Over the next forty-one years, dozens of explorers would outline the map of the Canadian Arctic, unravel the mystery of the Northwest Passage, and dispel many of the myths of the North. In a sense, Franklin's journey bracketed this period. He was on the first Arctic foray, and the golden age ended when Francis Leopold McClintock returned to Britain in 1859 with conclusive news of the ultimate fate of John Franklin's last expedition.

After Buchan and Ross returned, the navy moved rapidly to build on what meagre results the two expeditions had brought back. Attention moved away from the Pole – there was obviously no way through there – and settled firmly on the Northwest Passage. Here the British could fill in a huge blank area on the map, describe countless new species of animals and plants, and measure the mysterious magnetic phenomena.

The navy planned another dual attack. One route was obvious. Parry had come back expressing doubts about his commander's conclusion that Lancaster Sound was a dead end. That needed to be checked out, and Parry was given command this time. But what of the other expedition, now that the Pole had proved unattainable? What about an overland assault through the Canadian wilderness to the Arctic coast? That appeared to offer promise, and Samuel Hearne and Alexander Mackenzie had proved it was possible. For some unrecorded reason, the navy overlooked Buchan as leader, and offered command of the overland expedition to John Franklin.

The year 1818 marked the end of Franklin's apprenticeship. He was thirty-two years old, and he had a wealth of experience in both exploration and battle. He had proved himself calm in a crisis, and he was a popular leader. He had developed some strong navigational skills, he was a thorough observer with an interest in scientific inquiry, and he stood out from the horde of unemployed naval officers around him. He had challenged the Arctic and it was calling him back. John Franklin was ready to lead an expedition into unknown territory. He was about to begin the fabled quest for the Northwest Passage with which his name would be associated forever.

National Archives of Canada, C40327.

The place where Franklin's journey almost ended. Fort Enterprise under construction, 1820.

5

On the Route of the Voyageurs

"...we had the alarming view of a barren rugged shore within a few yards, towering over the mast-head. Almost instantly afterwards the ship struck violently on a point of rocks...On the outward bow was perceived a rugged and precipitous cliff, whose summit was hid in the fog...There now seemed to be no probability of escaping shipwreck..."

Franklin's *Narrative*, August 7, 1819

After hurried preparations, Franklin's small flotilla of three ships sailed for the unknown Canadian north on May 28, 1819. His first port of call was Yarmouth on the south coast of England. A sudden change of the wind caused them to sail at short notice, leaving behind one of the explorers, midshipman George Back. Upset at being left behind, Back made an extraordinary overland journey of nine days to rejoin the ships at Stromness in the Orkney Islands. It would not be his last remarkable journey on this expedition.

Fifty-three strenuous days later, on August 7, the explorers arrived at the entrance to Hudson Bay. Franklin's ship, *The Prince of Wales*, was promptly caught in a gale and driven onto the rocks of Resolution Island. The impact knocked the rudder out of position and the vessel was blown helplessly along the shore. Everyone assumed they were doomed. Miraculously, when *The Prince of Wales* grounded again, the rudder was knocked back into position and the crew gratefully managed to maneuvere the ship into deeper water. After two days of frantic work on the pumps, the ship's leaks were repaired and the voyage continued.

The next day, in Hudson Strait, Franklin met his first Canadian Inuit, or Esquimaux as they were called in those days. Only the previous year, in nearby Davis Strait, John Ross had described an encounter with Inuit who believed his ship to be alive because they had mistaken the sails for wings flapping in the wind. However, the members of the band Franklin encountered were used to fur trading ships passing that way. Around 150 men and women came out in a variety of boats to barter. Franklin was impressed with the quality of the walrus tusk carvings offered, the odd practice of licking trade goods to seal a deal, and by the orderly manner in which exchanges were made.

At last, on August 30, fourteen weeks after leaving London, the eventful journey was completed, and the *Prince of Wales* arrived at York Factory on the western shores of Hudson Bay. Franklin's luck was holding, but he was still more than four thousand kilometres from the beginning of his explorations.

The goal of Franklin's expedition was to map the Arctic coast of Canada, east from the mouth of the Coppermine River, which had been reached by Samuel Hearne in 1771. That point and the mouth of the Mackenzie River to the west were the only two locations on the coast ever previously visited by Europeans. Franklin was also charged with the important tasks of studying the natural history, examining the aurora, and taking detailed readings of all aspects of magnetic force.

Franklin was accompanied by a naturalist, Dr. John Richardson; two midshipmen, (the resourceful George Back and Robert Hood) to record the scientific data, conduct much of the navigation work, and draw and paint the landscape; and able seaman John Hepburn, who was assigned to be Franklin's personal servant. The British party was to be transported and supported by voyageurs of the Hudson's Bay and North West Companies and the Aboriginal Peoples living in the areas they were to explore.

Nineteen days before Franklin set off, Parry had sailed for Lancaster Sound to check whether Ross's assessment had been correct. The failure of the two 1818 adventures had not dulled all the optimism about Arctic travel, and the British Admiralty hoped that Franklin and Parry would meet somewhere in the wilderness. They never came within seven hundred kilometres of each other, but Parry was successful in exploring Prince Regent Inlet and reaching farther west than anyone else along the south shore of Melville Island. His became the first modern expedition to winter in the High Arctic.

Eager to be under way, Franklin and his party left York Factory on September 9, 1819. Their boat was too large and cumbersome for river travel and proved much slower than the lighter canoes of the voyageurs. Doggedly, Franklin pushed on, with Back and Hood mapping the route and sketching whenever they could, and Richardson collecting all manner of plant and animal life.

After crossing an opaque, clay-rich body of water, Franklin recorded a tale of how the lake had been given its name. A mischievous deity, Weesakootchaht, was once tricked and captured by an old woman. She called all the women of the First Nations band to come and punish Weesakootchaht for his tricks, and when he managed to escape he was so dirty that it took all the waters of the lake to clean him. Ever since, the lake had been called Winnipeg, or Muddy Water.

As they progressed laboriously up the Saskatchewan River, the weather became increasingly colder. Ice formed on the oars, making them difficult to handle; snow fell, and the oarsmen, who had to frequently immerse themselves in the river to manhandle the boat over rocks, suffered horribly in permanently wet and frozen clothes. At last, on October 23, 1819, 1110 kilometres and forty-four days from York Factory, they reached Cumberland House on the Saskatchewan River.

Richardson saw the local Cree as liars and boasters who tended to be "vain, fickle, improvident, and indolent," although he admitted that "they strictly regard the rights of property, are susceptible of the kinder affections, capable of friendship, very hospitable, tolerably kind to their women, and withal inclined to peace." Despite this patronizing attitude, Richardson was fascinated by the local culture. On one occasion, dressed in his naval uniform, he crouched in a smoke-filled tent and watched a tattooing ceremony. Both men and women endured the agony of having willow-charcoal rubbed into complex puncture wounds and charcoal-laden cord drawn through holes in their skin to produce dark patterns and lines. The tent was crowded and loud singing filled the air, as much, Richardson thought, to hide the groans of the victims as for religious reasons.

ꝏ

In mid-January of 1820, Franklin, Back, and Hepburn set off for the North West Company's post at Fort Chipewyan on Lake Athabasca to prepare for the following summer's work. They travelled with light sleds and on snowshoes, which they found difficult to master. After a harsh and exhausting journey, in temperatures that were sometimes cold enough to freeze the Englishmen's tea before they could drink it, the party arrived at Fort Chipewyan on March 26th. They had covered 1379 kilometres, almost all on foot.

At the fort, Franklin wasted no time arranging for supplies and men for the coming season. It was not easy; voyageurs did not want to travel north to where the Esquimaux, who had recently attacked and murdered the occupants of two trading canoes, lived, and food was scarce because many of the Cree hunters had been stricken with measles and whooping cough. The situation was made worse by the outright hostility exhibited between members of the North West Company and the Hudson's Bay Company. Both had agreed to help Franklin, but they were often so absorbed in their own trading war that they could not do much. These problems concerned Franklin, but in the noble imperial spirit of the time, he decided to press on regardless and do what he had been asked to do.

Franklin had a canoe made for the summer travel. It was ten metres long, almost 1.5 metres wide, and was composed of seventy-three hoops of cedar. The canoe was flimsy, but it could carry five or six men and provisions totalling 1497 kilograms. The canoe itself weighed 136 kilograms, but two voyageurs could carry it at a run over most portages.

Eventually Franklin collected enough men and supplies, and on July 13, Richardson and Hood rejoined the group. Five days later, they headed north for Great Slave Lake.

Summer travel turned out to be no easier than winter: camps were flooded, rapids damaged the canoes and made long portages necessary, and mosquitoes nearly drove the men insane. The voyageurs entertained Franklin's men by telling them graphic stories of previous disasters at places with such picturesque names as the Portage of the Drowned.

After ten days' travel, Franklin's party reached Fort Providence on the shores of Great Slave Lake. There, with flags flying and bedecked in their finest dress uniforms, the British officers strode forward to formally meet Akaitcho, or Big-foot, a local chief of the Copper (Yellowknife) First Nation who had agreed to help the explorers, and Frederick Wentzel, who had lived in the area for many years and was to act as a go-between. Akaitcho agreed to supply hunters and guides for Franklin and suggested a site for their winter base. Fort Providence was the most northerly trading outpost, so when the party set off on August 2, they were venturing into land previously visited by only one European, Samuel Hearne.

The party now consisted of twenty-eight persons, including the wives of three of the voyageurs and their three children. Amongst their bulky provisions, they carried gunpowder and shot, muskets, nails, cloth, blankets, and fishing nets. Their food included dried soup, flour, two cases of chocolate, tea, and two hundred dried reindeer tongues. Akaitcho's band went on ahead to hunt.

The cumbersome group travelled slowly and the shortage of provisions created some worrying moments early on. The voyageurs, who were doing all the hard work and consequently required vast amounts of food to maintain their energy levels (the fur industry standard was 3.5 kilograms of fresh meat per man per day), rebelled and refused to continue unless they were fed more. Franklin took a firm stand and threatened to blow out the brains of the first man to show any insubordination. This was treatment more usually offered to the pressed men on navy warships, and it must have come as something of a shock to the contract employees of the Canadian fur trade. Nonetheless, in the face of such a threat, the voyageurs continued, albeit with obvious bad grace.

Fortunately, some Yellowknife hunters arrived in the nick of time with some recently killed deer. After this, things settled down and the hunting improved. However, next fall the same problems – slow travel, inadequate supplies, and internal dissension – would resurface. Then there would be no happy ending.

On Sunday, August 20, 890 kilometres from Fort Chipewyan, the explorers arrived at their wintering site. Franklin named the place Fort Enterprise and immediately set to work building winter quarters. While his men worked, Franklin made plans to venture down the Coppermine River and prepare the way for the next season's travel. With an early winter looming, Akaitcho was reluctant to help. He told Franklin that he would supply men, but that he regarded the journey as a suicide mission and would begin mourning rituals as soon as the party left. Franklin was forced to compromise and settle for a much shorter trip, but the argument created a climate of distrust between the two men.

The party spent September hunting, fishing, preparing skins for blankets, making snowshoes, and building the two log houses in which they would live for nine months. Caribou were plentiful as they migrated south, and the men often saw as many as two thousand in a single day. They slaughtered and stored almost two hundred of the beasts. The fishing too was successful, supplying twelve hundred whitefish to the store. The Europeans were surprised to see the fish freeze as they were taken from the lake, but come back to life when they thawed, sometimes as much as thirty-six hours after they had been caught.

On October 18, Back, Wentzel and several Yellowknife warriors set off for Forts Providence and Chipewyan to hurry along the supplies which were supposed to be following the group. Most importantly, they needed to replenish their ammunition, which had been used up in the hunting, and their tobacco, without which the voyageurs would not work. Back was gone for five months. He travelled an extraordinary 1770 kilometres in deep winter, with insufficient food and in temperatures of -40 degrees. Despite the conditions, he set a winter travel record of ten days from Moose Deer Island to Fort Chipewyan. It was a remarkable achievement, but it did not help the party much. Supplies were either unavailable or in much smaller quantities than had been promised. Back returned empty-handed.

The search for supplies may not have been the only reason for sending midshipman Back to Fort Chipewyan. That fall Back and Hood both fell in love with the daughter of one of the Yellowknife guides.

Called "Greenstockings" because of her dress, she so captivated the two young Englishmen that they developed a strong rivalry. They became so jealous of each other that they agreed to a duel to settle the matter, and Hepburn, fearing the worst, surreptitiously removed the charges from the two men's pistols. To defuse the situation, Franklin sent Back off to chase up the supplies.

With Back out of the way, Hood continued to court Greenstockings. He painted her picture and spent much time in her company. Hood died the following year, but a census taken at Fort Resolution in 1823 records the existence of, "the orphaned daughter of Lieutenant Hood."

Through the winter, occasional small quantities of supplies reached Fort Enterprise, the most popular being casks of rum. Life settled into a routine, with the officers working on their journals and maps, taking scientific readings, and collecting and describing specimens of the local flora and fauna, and the men cutting wood for the fires. Even with fires burning constantly in the living quarters, the temperature dropped to -15 degrees inside and a low of -57 degrees outside.

By early spring of 1821, the fall kill of meat was all gone and Franklin was forced to break into the supplies of preserved meat he had been saving for the summer's exploration. Despite rationing, this food too was almost gone by April, and the party was forced to subsist on irregular hunting successes. Akaitcho and his band returned, but the chief's attitude to Franklin had been soured by their disagreements. Franklin had to work hard to assert what he saw as his authority and force Akaitcho to supply the promised hunters and guides.

By mid-June, despite a shortage of supplies and caches of meat destroyed by wolverines, Franklin was ready to go. Through June and July, he led his party down the Coppermine River, retracing Samuel Hearne's route. Some game was killed, but it was not enough. The voyageurs' legs swelled, a sure sign that they were not getting enough calories for their gruelling work.

Near the site where Hearne had described a bloody massacre of the Inuit by the Yellowknives, Franklin also encountered Inuit. Despite repeated attempts at contact, and the presence of interpreters, they proved elusive and rapidly withdrew when Franklin's men approached. However, this contact with the Inuit scared the Yellowknife guides and hunters, and they decided to return home, seriously reducing Franklin's ability to secure sufficient food through hunting.

Finally, on the evening of July 18, 1821, Franklin caught a glimpse of dark rolling waves dotted with white patches of ice. At last, after two years and two months of arduous travel, he was standing where Samuel Hearne had stood fifty years before – on the shore of the Arctic Ocean. The North had pulled Franklin back to the very limit of the known world, but his journey was not over yet. Hearne had taken a quick look and returned up the river. Franklin would go on, along the coast and into the real unknown.

The following day Wentzel and four voyageurs returned to Fort Enterprise with strict instructions to make sure adequate supplies of food were left there for the returning party. The group of twenty men who remained were tired, underfed, short of supplies, short of skilled hunters, and unsure that their line of retreat was secure. But even though Franklin was adrift in the wilderness, he felt a great sense of relief. He was on his own now, free from arguing fur traders, recalcitrant natives, or petty squabbles over love affairs – there was simply the Arctic coast, stretching ahead and waiting for John Franklin to make his mark. It was a heady moment, but the explorers had not escaped their past difficulties, which would soon resurface to claim the lives of eleven men.

6

Along the Arctic Coast

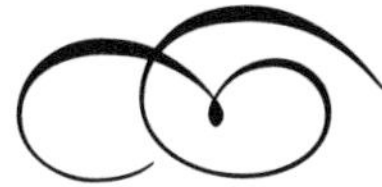

"...Dr. Richardson came in to communicate the joyful intelligence that relief had arrived...poor Adam was in so low a state that he could scarcely comprehend the information...But for this seasonable interposition of Providence, his existence must have terminated in a few hours, and that of the rest probably in not many days."

Franklin's *Narrative*, November 7, 1821

Franklin's venture along the coast began inauspiciously. For one-and-a-half days he had to sit in a wind-battered tent while strong winds whipped the sea into a frenzy. Finally, at noon on July 21, the elements

National Archives of Canada, C102851.

The hazards of mapping an unknown coast. Landing in a storm, 1821.

calmed, and with less than fifteen days supply of food and enough powder and shot for one thousand charges, John Franklin set off into the unknown.

At first the coast was smooth and the going easy, but soon it became more rugged and ice threatened to trap them against the shore. On July 24 they killed a caribou and feasted. Two days later they narrowly escaped being crushed rounding Cape Barrow. Ice, wind, and fog slowed them frustratingly and game was scarce. Slowly they ate into their meagre preserved supplies. Meticulous mapping of the tortuous coastline around Arctic Sound, Bathurst Inlet, and Melville Sound cost them days, and each time they ended up almost back where they had begun. Franklin's hope of speeding through to Hudson Bay that season vanished.

One of Franklin's problems was that he had two conflicting tasks to perform. First, he was to map the unknown coast. Second, he was to ascertain the orientation of the coast between the Coppermine River and Hudson Bay. To do one, he had to carefully map each indentation in the coastline. To do the other, he had to skip across the mouths of inlets and hurry east as fast as he could. Being the first to travel that way, he had no way of knowing, when the coast turned and began to trend south, whether this was another inlet, or the main coast. Was the blur of land in the distance an island or the mainland where it swung back? The only way to find out was to go and see, and that took time.

On August 15, with only three days' food left and no contact made with the Inuit, Franklin made a decision. They would struggle on until the coast trended eastwards or for four days, whichever came first. On

August 18, Franklin, Richardson, and Back left the canoes and walked on for twenty kilometres. The coast ahead appeared to trend to the east. Franklin named the spot Point Turnagain and began his disastrous retreat to Fort Providence. They had mapped over one thousand kilometres of coastline for a gain of little more than two hundred as the crow flies.

The way back along the coast would be easier, since it was known ground and they could cut across the mouths of previously mapped inlets and bays. After being held up by gales for four days, they managed to reach the mouth of Hood River in another four, a journey that had taken them more than two weeks in the other direction. Here Franklin made another decision – one that, combined with the problems of supply and local ignorance that had been compounding almost from the beginning, sealed the fate of over half his party.

Franklin knew that there was precious little game along the coast back to the Coppermine. He also knew that their hunting had been quite good at Hood River. He decided to cut across country back to Fort Enterprise. On the map, the route didn't look too bad, 240 kilometres in a straight line, but Franklin ignored one thing – the Yellowknife people avoided the barren lands as much as possible, sticking close to rivers and lakes in their travel. This local knowledge should have carried more weight with someone who was low on supplies, late in the season, and facing more than two hundred kilometres of barren lands travel.

The reason Akaitcho's people avoided the barren lands soon became apparent. The rough ground was torture on the feet of men carrying heavy loads and wearing only thin moccasins. Rivers and lakes obstructed their journey, causing detours and delays and almost killing them during crossings. Nothing broke the force of the cruel, wind-driven snow as it whipped against the starving men. At a snail-like pace, the weak, overburdened men struggled through the snow, one agonizing step at a time. They could not remove their frozen clothes at night. They slept on top of their boots so the boots would not freeze and could be worn for the next day's gruelling march. During the day, they paused only to collect *Tripe de Roche*, a lichen that grows on the bare rocks north of the tree-line. The lichen was their main source of food and, for working men, it was hopelessly inadequate. Apart from lacking nutritional value, *Tripe de Roche* often produces violent stomach cramps. One of Franklin's party, midshipman Robert Hood, was so badly afflicted that he could eat nothing and weakened rapidly.

On September 10 one of the hunters shot a muskox. "This success infused spirit into our starving party. To skin and cut up the animal was the work of a few minutes. The contents of its stomach were devoured upon the spot, and the raw intestines, which were next attacked, were pronounced by the most delicate amongst us to be excellent."

Every delay at a river crossing or detour around a lake cost the starving men precious time. Their trail became marked by discarded scientific specimens and equipment. At the end of September they reached the Coppermine River, only sixty-four kilometres from Fort Enterprise. Their canoe had long since been abandoned, so John Richardson, the expedition naturalist, attempted to swim a line through the frigid waters of the rapids. Halfway over, he lost all feeling in his arms and legs and sank from view. Hauling frantically, his companions pulled him back, more dead than alive. They stripped him, wrapped him in blankets and laid him before the fire. Richardson recovered, but it was several months before feeling returned to the left side of his body. The rapids on the Coppermine cost them nine days.

Midshipman George Back and three of the strongest men went ahead to Fort Enterprise to secure supplies. The rest struggled on as best they could. The weakest fell behind and froze to death. No one was strong enough to help them. Eventually Hood became so weak he couldn't continue. Richardson and Able Seaman Hepburn set up a camp and stayed with him while Franklin pushed on. For four of Franklin's companions, the effort was too much, and they turned back to Richardson's camp. Only one of them, Michel, arrived.

On October 11, Franklin saw Fort Enterprise in the distance. It was silent. There was no activity around the fort, no smoke from the chimneys, and no sign of George Back. With a horrible sense of foreboding, Franklin stumbled on. The fort was deserted. Even worse, there were none of the promised supplies. The whole party broke down in tears.

Unable to continue or to go back, Franklin and the other survivors managed as best they could. On the evening of October 29, Richardson and Hepburn staggered into the bleak camp. They had a tale of unspeakable horror to tell.

Michel had arrived back alone and apparently worked hard to hunt and supply Richardson, Hood, and Hepburn with food. On one occasion he presented them with some wolf meat. But his behaviour became increasingly erratic. On Sunday, October 20, Richardson and Hepburn heard a musket shot. When they went to investigate, they found Hood dead. He had been shot at close range from behind and Michel could not explain how it had happened. Richardson and Hepburn became convinced that Michel had murdered Hood. They also began to suspect that the "wolf meat" was human flesh, cut from the frozen bodies of the others who had left Franklin's party and who Michel had murdered. It became obvious that Michel was planning to kill them. Richardson and Hepburn determined to act first.

Worried that they were so weak that they would not be able to resist an attack by Michel, they decided that their only hope was in killing the stronger man. Hepburn volunteered to carry out the execution, but Richardson knew that, as senior officer, it was his responsibility. The two men waited for their chance. It came when Michel dropped behind to hunt. Richardson met him as he returned and "put an end to his life by shooting him through the head with a pistol."

After Richardson and Hepburn arrived at Fort Enterprise, the health of the party continued to decline. They often saw game close to the fort, but rarely had the strength to hunt. The most meagre success was greeted with rejoicing: "Hepburn having shot a partridge, which was brought to the house, the Doctor [John Richardson] tore out the feathers, and having held it in the fire a few minutes, divided it into seven portions. Each piece was ravenously devoured by my companions, as it was the first morsel of flesh any of us had tasted for thirty-one days, unless indeed the small gristly particles which we found occasionally adhering to the pounded bones may be termed flesh."

On November 1, two more men died of starvation. Now only Franklin, Richardson, Hepburn, and one other man clung to a precarious flicker of life, dreaming of food and arguing pointlessly about nothing.

By November 7, Richardson and Hepburn heard the musket shot that signalled salvation. Eleven of the twenty who explored the coast were dead. Slowly the survivors headed south. On December 3 they had the "indescribable gratification" of changing the tattered clothes they had worn solidly since the end of August. In the spring of 1822 they boarded a ship for home.

It was an ordeal of epic proportions, and Franklin was very lucky to survive. But was he to blame? Certainly there were factors beyond his control. The British navy had no experience organizing overland expeditions. Self-contained seaborne expeditions were its forte, and the navy did not fully understand problems of travelling overland. The preparation time was too short to iron out all the problems. Franklin could have objected, but given his personality and the times, he was unlikely to. Franklin was a gentle, calm man, capable of being firm when he thought it necessary, but not one to make waves with higher authority. In addition, in 1819 there were hundreds of out-of-work junior naval officers, any one of whom would jump in eagerly if Franklin were seen as being a problem and were pushed aside.

The timing too was unfortunate. The rivalry between the Hudson's Bay Company and the North West Company was at its height. In their attempts to control the incredibly lucrative fur trade, both companies had no qualms about supplying whisky to the native hunters, destroying the opposition's trading posts, traplines, and caches of supplies, and ambushing – sometimes even killing – opposing voyageurs. Both companies agreed to help Franklin, but the circumstances, added to the diseases sweeping the First Nations' hunting population, meant that even traders with the best will in the world could do little to help. They were having a hard enough time feeding their own men.

Finally, the weather was against him. His first winter at Fort Enterprise was relatively benign. The second, which caught his party exposed on the barrens just as they were beginning their retreat from the coast, was harsh, and it set in abruptly, weeks earlier than usual. The early onset of winter drove away what game there was and seriously weakened the travelling men.

Although Franklin's personal luck remained intact and ensured his survival, overall, his first expedition was an unlucky venture. Nevertheless, it should not have been the disaster it was. Franklin's biggest mistake was in ignoring the supply problems around him. From the beginning, things did not go as planned and there was a shortage of food. Franklin saw the problems and appreciated that they were not going to improve, putting his party at risk during the summer of exploration when margins for error were at their slimmest. Whether he naively believed things would somehow work themselves out, or whether he, like Scott at the South Pole ninety years later, was driven on past the point of rationality by a desire to accomplish great things and perform his duty, is not known. Certainly Franklin was a product of his time in that he had a high regard for authority and believed in the early nineteenth-century ideals of Honour, Courage, and Nobility. It is difficult from our more cynical perspective almost two centuries later to appreciate how strongly Franklin's class felt these things. People were willing to die for Honour. In 1821, Franklin very nearly did.

Given his supply problems, Franklin had to rely very heavily on the local native population and the voyageurs. The problem here was that he was culturally incapable of understanding or appreciating their advice. Useful though these people were for carrying loads, chopping firewood, and hunting, they were lesser beings without the refined tastes or religious convictions of an upper class Englishman. This didn't mean that Franklin was a racist, he felt much the same way about a poverty-stricken millworker from Birmingham, and he had no wish to hurt anyone. More accurately, his attitude was an arrogant paternalism. Given the right circumstances and enough time, these people might one day achieve something close to the great cultural benefits Franklin himself enjoyed. The problem in the short term was that Franklin's attitude made him think less of the locals' opinions than his own or those of his fellow officers, despite the fact that British sailors could know nothing of the land in which the voyageurs and Akaitcho and his people lived and thrived.

Franklin's cultural arrogance is not one of his most endearing characteristics and illustrates his great weakness, an inability to stand outside his cultural prejudices, even when circumstances obviously demanded it. In his narrative of the journey, Franklin describes his party's arrival at the Arctic coast. He ridicules the voyageurs' expressions of concern over the suitability of the canoes for sea travel, the quantity of available food, and the dangers of travel over the barren lands. Franklin wrote this months after the canoes proved unsuitable, food could not be obtained, and travel over the barren lands had killed half his party. Even when lesser mortals were dramatically and tragically proved correct, a man of Franklin's class and culture could not afford to acknowledge that they had been right. What is remarkable is not that the voyageurs let Franklin down as he asserts in his narrative, but that they stayed by him so long and helped him get as far as he did in the face of his overbearing attitude.

Had Franklin somehow managed to slip the constraints of his cultural heritage, what could he have done? Short of abandoning virtually everything an Englishman of his day knew and believed in and mounting a small, rapidly moving, live-off-the-land-like-the-locals-do expedition a century ahead of its time, his only option in the circumstances he faced was to abandon the exploration goals and return home. He was not about to do that. Failure without the evidence of having nobly struggled forward to the last extremity would have spelled disaster for his career. Whispers that he was not made of the "right stuff" would have doomed him to retirement on half pay if not outright disgrace. The Royal Navy was John Franklin's life; he would be a broken man without it. What was the risk of death for him and his companions compared to that?

After the horrors of the barren lands, the return trip to England was easy. It was slow, as the sick men gradually recovered their strength, but largely uneventful.

When Franklin returned to Britain in 1822 he was greeted with jubilation. The public had a hero. A rather embarrassed Franklin was held up as a cultural ideal; the noble explorer winning through incredible hardships despite the weaknesses and treachery of the savages and half-caste voyageurs around him. Of course, the fact that the "half-caste voyageurs" had done all the hard work, that nine of the eleven voyageurs in the exploration party had died, and that the entire expedition would have died without the food supplied by the "savages" was conveniently forgotten. That didn't fit with the burgeoning imperial world view.

Paradoxically, the fact that the expedition had relied heavily on local food sources and local manpower to supply hunting skills and workers was held up as a serious flaw. The next expedition to the Canadian North, and most subsequent ones that century, would rely on the muscles of the sturdy British sailor to supply strength, and the intelligence and skill of the plucky British officer to supply leadership and hunting skills. Unfortunately, this worked so well on Franklin's second expedition that it entrenched the idea firmly and not even the horrific disaster of his third expedition dislodged it.

National Archives of Canada, C001352.

The returning hero who won Eleanor Porden's heart.
Portrait of John Franklin.

7

Romantic explorations

> "The question is not, my dear Sir, whether you and I can mutually esteem each other as friends, but whether we are calculated to live together in the closest domestic union.... There is yet one moment to hesitate and only one."
>
> Eleanor Porden to John Franklin, July, 1823

Back in the security of Britain, between accepting his honours, planning a new expedition, and writing up the volume of his previous exploits, Franklin found the time to resume his courtship of Eleanor Ann Porden, the young poet who had first visited his ship four-and-a-half years before as he prepared to set out for the North Pole with Buchan.

After his return from Spitzbergen, Franklin had become a frequent visitor at the Porden home, where the young Eleanor kept house for her invalid mother and father, the famous architect, William Porden. Apparently, Franklin even considered proposing marriage, but decided against it because of the dangers of the expedition he was undertaking. Nevertheless, Eleanor was not far from his mind in the far north and he named the Porden Islands near Point Turnagain for her.

Franklin was thirty-six in 1822 and Eleanor was eleven years his junior. She had a cultured upbringing and was interested in science and the arts. She surrounded herself with young, like-minded artists, who called themselves "The Attic Chest," and met on Sunday afternoons after church to discuss each other's literary work. These friends undoubtedly took their literary dabbling seriously, but Eleanor had some justification for doing so. At the age of sixteen, she had written "The Veils; or The Triumph of Constancy. A Poem in Six Books."

The work runs to almost three hundred pages and is a romantic treatment of scientific discovery. It was inspired by a series of lectures the young poet attended and the loss of her veil in a wind while she strolled on the beach one day. This poem seems overly romantic and very long-winded today, and it is filled with obscure literary and scientific references, but it was well received at the time.

> The Knight, in prime of youthful vigour, joined
> Undaunted courage, and a courteous mind;
> Black were his arms – the painting on his shield

The strange occasion of their grief revealed:
Lo ! on the foamy ocean's shingly sands,
Reft of her Veil, a weeping damsel stands,
Beside a yawning gulf a Gnome appears,
Who waves the ravished veil and mocks her tears;
While forms ethereal lightly float in air,
And weep in pity o'er the injured fair.

Because of this poem, Eleanor was admitted to the French Institute, a remarkable honour for a teenage girl in those days. Her father encouraged her to continue to write poetry.

One of Eleanor's young friends, Jane Griffin, wrote that "she makes all her own clothes, preserves, pickles, dances quadrilles *con amore*, belongs to a poetical book club, pays morning visits, sees all the sights, never denies herself to anybody at any hour, and lies in bed or is not dressed till nine o'clock in the morning." It is difficult to tell what of the above is intended as a compliment and what is not. Certainly Jane's physical description of Eleanor could have been kinder. She wrote that her friend was a, "plain, stout, short young woman, having a rather vulgar though very good-natured countenance." But then, Jane herself was a notable beauty.

Eleanor seems a strange choice for someone of Franklin's background. His was a life of action, with little time for cultural pursuits. They probably admired each other's achievements, but it is hard to imagine what they had in common to talk about. Whatever the reason, Franklin took the relationship seriously and proposed to Eleanor within two months of his return.

Eleanor had not considered marriage while she felt responsible for her father, but in 1822 he was dying and encouraged her to pick a husband. Whom this should be seems to have been a topic for debate and her literary group drew up a list of ten suitable names. The leading candidate appears to have been a Mr. Elliott, the private secretary to the British Prime Minister, Lord Palmerston. Elliott had much in common with Eleanor and they had been friends for many years. But Eleanor was determined to wait until Franklin returned from Canada. No one knows what happened between the players of this scene. Letters hint at undercurrents of emotion and doubt. Only a month before the wedding, Eleanor felt timid about the upcoming event. She wrote to Mr. Elliott that, "I sometimes feel as if I had in some respects made an odd choice." Elliott replied, "I hope and wish to become his friend for your sake."

Perhaps Franklin's proposal of marriage, coming as it did so soon after her father's death and in the midst of Franklin's fame as a returning hero, appealed to Eleanor's romantic sensibilities. Despite whatever misgivings she had, Eleanor accepted Franklin's proposal, and Mr. Elliott turned away to marry someone else.

John Franklin and Eleanor Porden were married on August 19, 1823. Differences between the two became apparent almost immediately. Eleanor set up their home in the house in which she had been born in

London. Here she could keep in touch with her literary friends and the arts scene in the city. Franklin's father had died in the spring of 1823, and John spent increased amounts of time in Spilsby.

Eleanor was not one to keep her opinions to herself. Franklin was deeply religious, refusing even to write letters on a Sunday. Eleanor and he had many misunderstandings and disagreements on this topic. On one occasion she told her new husband, "I cannot agree with you respecting Sunday.... Shall I tell you the truth? I have studied you much, and have thought that on some points of this subject you seemed to be guided by an impulse foreign to your general nature. Mild as you usually are, your looks and voice have actually terrified me, and the first time left an impression from which I cannot recover."

This suggests a level of anger in Franklin's temperament which is not seen elsewhere. He is universally portrayed as a gentle man. Eleanor's sister even called him that and criticized Eleanor for being too overbearing in forcing her opinions on John. Certainly, Franklin did not consider himself Eleanor's intellectual equal. He regarded her mind as "higher and more richly endowed" than his own. In response to her accusations of religious intolerance, he replied, "If I know my own heart I am no bigot on these points, but on the contrary am willing to permit everyone to cherish their own sentiments."

In June 1824, the couple had a daughter, Eleanor, a child "so like her father, that it's like looking at Captain Franklin through the wrong end of a telescope."

Family life did not bring the couple closer and they still spent much time apart, Eleanor in her house in London surrounded by her literary friends, and John either in Spilsby or arranging his return to the Canadian wilderness. What the birth of little Eleanor did do, however, was exacerbate her mother's illness.

Eleanor Franklin had consumption. Called pulmonary tuberculosis today, consumption was a major killer in the days before antibiotics. There was no cure. Neither of the Franklins seem to have taken the disease too seriously early in their marriage. "I am not very ill," Eleanor wrote in early 1824. But her condition deteriorated rapidly after her child was born, and by the end of the year she was bedridden. Even so, she tried to maintain her cheerfulness and encouraged Franklin to continue preparations for his upcoming expedition. The strain on Franklin was immense as he prepared for a major exploration while watching his wife die. He also received word that his brother, Willingham, had died of cholera in India. Jane Griffin recalled that Franklin was so preoccupied at this time that he did not reply to letters and notes or even acknowledge presents she sent him.

There was some gossip and scandal that Franklin should be preparing so assiduously to leave his dying wife, but it had always been their agreement that the marriage should not interfere with his career, and Eleanor was adamant: she wanted him to go. She stated strongly that his departure was not a factor in her worsening state. Indeed, when possible, Franklin kept vigil at his sick wife's bedside, and described her condition in one of his letters: "The disease has continued its rapid progress, and she is now to all appearance nearly at her last extremity; but such has been her muscular strength that she has rallied frequently, and it is not improbable that she may linger even through this day. I seize an interval of repose to commence this letter to you in this room, where I have been watching all the night."

Although at times it looked like she might not live to see her husband's departure, Eleanor did linger. She even showed some signs of improvement, and when Franklin said goodbye on February 16, 1825, he still had some faint hopes that she might recover.

On the evening of Friday, 22 April, 1825, on the shore of Lake Huron, Franklin composed a letter to Eleanor. Lightheartedly, he told her about the social circumstances at the naval station where he was staying. He described his visit to New York and wished she had been with him to see the industry of the Americans. After expressing his disappointment that there was not a letter waiting for him, he went on, "I shall embark, however, with every hope that the Almighty has been pleased to restore you to health before this, and that you are now in the enjoyment of every comfort. I daily remember you and our dear little one in our prayers, and I have no doubt yours are offered up on my behalf. She must be growing very entertaining, and I sincerely trust she will be a source of great comfort to us, especially to you in my absence. With what heartfelt pleasure shall I embrace you both on my return!... Mr. Back and the men have arrived..."

His letter stops here in mid-sentence. Mr. Back had brought the mail. At the bottom of the never-finished letter, Franklin scrawled in a shaky hand, "7 p.m. The distressing intelligence of my dear wife's death has just reached me."

Eleanor had only outlived Franklin's departure by six days. All the hopeful letters he had written in the previous two months had been addressed to a dead woman.

Franklin was distraught by the news and doubted if he could go on. Nevertheless, he was a pragmatist; he did continue, and the following summer he named Port Griffin at the mouth of the Mackenzie River for his dead wife's beautiful friend Jane.

8

Back to the Canadian Arctic

> "Not a murmur of discontent was heard throughout the voyage and every individual engaged with alacrity in the laborious tasks he was called up to perform...."
>
> Richardson on his eastern explorations

Franklin learned many lessons from the disasters of his first expedition. However, despite the unqualified success of his second expedition, he had, in fact, learned the wrong lessons.

The first expedition had failed largely due to the heavy reliance on uncertain local resources and on Franklin's cultural blindness, which made him unable to learn from the local aboriginal people and the

By permission, The Champlain Society.

Inuit pillaging the boats on Franklin's second expedition.

voyageurs who had the knowledge he needed to succeed. His response was not to change his attitude to the local experts and learn from them, but to eliminate them from the equation. This time around, Franklin would take everything he needed with him.

To the upper-class British officer of the early nineteenth century, Franklin's decision made sense. Don't rely on locals who do not have the advantages of a classical education and cannot quote anything in Latin or Greek. Franklin's success in 1826 appeared to confirm his decision. The second expedition was a model of good management, careful planning, and almost flawless execution. Ironically, the expedition's very success in relying solely on outside resources contained the seeds of much greater tragedy.

While Franklin had been struggling back across the barren lands, Edward Parry had also been busy. His voyage of 1819-1820 had been a great success. It had been followed by an attempt in 1821-1823 to force a passage out of Foxe Basin north of Hudson Bay. This voyage had discovered Fury and Hecla Strait and confirmed the idea that the entrance to the Northwest Passage was indeed Lancaster Sound. When Parry returned to Britain in 1823, he immediately proposed a third assault on the Passage. Franklin had been back since the end of 1822, and he enthusiastically supported the venture, proposing another overland expedition to complement Parry's nautical one.

The Admiralty was keen on both and again hoped the explorers might meet. This hope was even more wildly off than before. Parry sailed in 1824 to explore Prince Regent Inlet. After wintering there, one of his two ships, the *Fury*, was damaged and had to be abandoned. The supplies she carried were cached ashore at Fury Beach, and the explorers returned home in October 1825. As they did so, Franklin and his party were just settling in to their winter quarters at Fort Franklin on the shores of Great Bear Lake.

On his second trip to the Canadian North, Franklin was accompanied again by Richardson and Back. He got on well with Richardson and was glad to have him along, but the brash young George Back was not his first choice. Neither Richardson nor Franklin was keen to have Back on the second expedition, and Franklin only accepted him when pressured by the Admiralty after the man who was his first choice had inconveniently died. Back was probably too outspoken and arrogant for Franklin's quiet temperament, but he was undoubtedly a superb traveller. Had he not been, Franklin and Richardson would not have survived to undertake a second expedition at all.

With the three officers went Mate E. N. Kendall as assistant surveyor, Thomas Drummond as assistant naturalist, and four Royal Marines. They were preceded by several sailors and marines who were to prepare the way for the main party. Rather than rely on birch bark canoes, which had been a problem on the open Arctic sea, Franklin had three wooden boats specially made. Each could carry twenty-two men and eight tonnes of supplies. He also commissioned a small folding craft, called the walnut-shell from its shape, so that the delays at river crossings could be avoided.

Instead of a few months, Franklin had a full year to make preparations this time, and he used it to the full. Supplies and equipment, including the new boats and two carpenters, were shipped out ahead of the party and stored at Hudson's Bay Company posts along the way. By 1825, the Hudson's Bay Company had merged with the North West Company, ending the rivalry which had made things difficult in 1821. Franklin was additionally fortunate in securing the services of Peter Warren Dease, Chief Factor with the Hudson's Bay Company, to organize supplies for him in Canada and fill the role Frederick Wentzel had played on the first expedition.

By February 1825 all was ready. Taking a silk flag Eleanor had made for him to unfurl on the shores of the Arctic sea, Franklin said goodbye to his dying wife and sailed for North America. The ocean voyage and the trip across Canada had none of the drama of the previous one. Everything worked like clockwork, and Franklin astonished the local company men by arriving at Fort Chipewyan in mid-July. By the beginning of August, they had reached Great Bear Lake.

This time around, there was time for Franklin to scout ahead and there was no annoying Akaitcho to say "no." On August 7, Franklin, Kendall, and a boat crew set off down the Mackenzie River to have a look at the Arctic Sea. Nine days later, the party reached salt water and were excited by the sight of the sea "in all its majesty, entirely free from ice," and with "many seals and black and white whales...sporting on its waves." The small group pitched a tent, gave three cheers, and unfurled the flag Eleanor had made. It was an intensely emotional moment for Franklin, but he felt it was his duty to hide the way he felt so as not to minimize the joy of his companions. Optimistically leaving a note for Parry, Franklin stayed only one night before hurrying back up the river to his winter quarters.

The winter at Fort Franklin was a much more enjoyable experience than the one at Fort Enterprise. Despite the fact that there were sometimes more than fifty people around the fort, food was never a problem. By fishing and hunting the men laid in a good supply of frozen meat and they added to this stock throughout the cold months. Each officer had his own private room in a building measuring thirteen by seven metres. The men were a bit more cramped. Twenty or thirty of them lived in a building eleven by seven metres but, at least according to the officers, spirits were high. The men received schooling in reading, writing, and arithmetic and participated in games and dances to help combat boredom. Sixty people attended the Christmas party. It was a raucous occasion, with songs and speech in English, Scots Gaelic, French, Inuit, and Chipewyan, Dogrib and Hare dialects, and music provided by fiddle and bagpipes.

In the new year, Peter Dease's wife gave birth to a daughter. The explorers celebrated with a feast consisting of boiled and roasted fish, accompanied by fish soup and a bottle of preserved peppers. There was no bread since the mice had eaten the flour. The diet was undoubtedly limited, but there was always enough.

As spring progressed, they prepared for that summer's exploration. Two parties were to set out, both from the mouth of the Mackenzie River. Franklin, Back, eleven sailors and marines, two voyageurs, and one interpreter would take two boats and map the coast to the west and possibly meet up with a ship, commanded by Franklin's old companion Beechey, that was to sail along the coast from the Bering Strait. Richardson and ten men would map to the east as far as the mouth of the Coppermine River and then return to Great Bear Lake.

By July 4, the two parties were at the mouth of the Mackenzie and ready to go their separate ways. There was a world of difference between this occasion and the first expedition. Then, Franklin was in charge of an unhappy, squabbling group of tired men, with very little food and unsuitable canoes. Now he was accompanied by fit, enthusiastic sailors who would never question his orders. He had custom-designed boats, the best equipment available, a wealth of presents for the Inuit he hoped to encounter, and food enough for three months. What could go wrong?

In fact, very little did go wrong. The only time Franklin's party was in danger was just after they had begun. On July 7, Franklin spotted an Inuit encampment on shore. Approaching to trade, the Europeans' boats were soon surrounded by dozens of kayaks whose owners eagerly offered everything they had. Fearing that the situation might get out of control, Franklin ordered his boats to pull off to deeper water. Unfortunately, the falling tide stranded them high and dry. More Inuit arrived until there were 250 to 300 men, women, and children swarming the boats.

Overcome by the sight of all the treasures in the boats, some of the Inuit became aggressive. They climbed in beside the sailors, waving knives and cutting buttons off jackets. One man had to tie the vital astronomical instruments to his leg to prevent them being carried away. Anything not tied down was spirited over the side of the boat and disappeared in the milling throng. With incredible patience, the sailors refrained from reacting violently to the provocation, and for several hours they struggled to keep their weapons and vital equipment.

Eventually, the tide returned and the sailors were able to refloat the boats. To discourage pursuit, Franklin ordered his men to level their muskets at the Inuit. The Inuit withdrew. Franklin was full of praise for the restraint shown by his sailors. It was a tense situation which, like many other European/Native encounters, could easily have turned into a tragedy with just one wrong move. No one had been killed or wounded and the Inuit had stolen mostly trade goods in any case. They had taken some canteens, kettles, a tent, blankets, shoes, and sails, but the vital instruments had been saved. Naming the site Pillage Point, Franklin camped for the night.

The following morning, the Inuit again approached in their kayaks. The leader waved one of the kettles and shouted that he wanted to return it. Not wishing a repeat of the previous day's swarming, Franklin declined the offer, fired a musket shot across the kayak's bows to make his point, and sailed on along the coast. In succeeding days, Franklin met other Inuit groups and managed to establish friendly and mutually profitable relationships. He was even told that the Inuit close to the mouth of the Mackenzie had a bad reputation.

ꝏ

After Franklin had survived his encounters with the human occupants of the Arctic coast, he had only the elements to contend with. Intermittently held up by fog, ice, and wind, he worked his way west, mapping the coast as he went. It was tedious work.

On July 27, the party crossed into Russian territory. On August 16, after being held up for a week at a depressing place Franklin christened Foggy Island, it became clear they would have to turn back. Although it was at that time only 240 kilometres away, Franklin would not meet up with Beechey's ship from the Bering Strait. The season was advanced and the men were suffering from the hard work and continued exposure to freezing water. On August 17, Franklin turned back.

The return journey was marked by severe storms and several friendly encounters with Inuit. On one occasion, Franklin recognized an Inuit man who had been present when the boats had been swarmed. He told Franklin that the intention had been to overwhelm the boats and kill all the occupants. On another occasion, two Inuit arrived with a story that a band of strangers from the mountains were close by and intended to kill the intruders as they believed them to be a threat to their trade. The Inuit urged Franklin's men to leave.

On September 21, Franklin's party arrived back at Fort Franklin. Richardson had returned safely on September 1 and left again to collect geological samples around Great Slave Lake. Both parties had done well. Franklin had travelled 3295 kilometres and mapped 981 kilometres of previously unexplored coast. Richardson had covered 3186 kilometres including 1633 kilometres of unexplored territory.

Richardson had been favoured with better weather than Franklin had, and the only problems he had faced were with Inuit who threatened to overwhelm his small boats. Like Franklin, he had used the threat of muskets to defuse the situation. Richardson had also made an extensive collection of botanical specimens.

The explorers settled into their winter routine. In February, Franklin, five sailors, and two local guides left the fort and began the long journey home. Travelling from trading post to trading post, he reached Cumberland House on June 18. There he met Richardson, who had travelled to the west to meet with the assistant naturalist Drummond. Drummond had not gone north, but had led a solitary existence collecting specimens across the prairies towards the Rocky Mountains. Between June 1825 and April 1827, he had collected 1500 species of plants, 150 birds, 50 quadrupeds, and hundreds of insects.

Franklin has often been criticized for the slow, ponderous nature of his expeditions. Light, fast parties living off the land could have accomplished more exploration in a shorter time. This is true, but they could not have collected the scientific data that Richardson and Drummond did. One-third of Franklin's two substantial books on his expeditions consist of scientific appendices. There are notes on topography, geology, and meteorology; data on magnetic variations, the aurora, the speed of sound, and solar radiation; and there are zoological descriptions and drawings and lists of animals, fishes, insects, and a staggering total of 633 plants. Franklin was slow, but he was methodical, and his explorations contributed a considerable body of information to the scientific knowledge of the day.

From Cumberland House, Franklin and Richardson undertook a leisurely journey home, setting aside time for social visits in Montreal and New York. They arrived back in Liverpool on September 26 after an absence of slightly over two-and-a-half years. Back and the others Franklin had left on Great Bear Lake arrived home two weeks later.

Franklin's second expedition was an unqualified success. The pattern was set for the future: take all necessary supplies and don't rely on uncertain local resources. Unfortunately, a possible consequence of this approach is overconfidence. The risk becomes one of blundering into a situation where technology, supplies, and expertise are of no use. That is exactly what would happen on Franklin's third expedition, but he had to wait almost two decades to find that out.

National Portrait Gallery, London, Reg. No. 904 Date: 1816. Artist: Amélie Romilly.

Beautiful and strong-willed. Jane Franklin contemplates how best to advance her husband's career.

9

Russia to Greece

> "I should rejoice to see with you the same things for the first time, to help or be helped by you in every little difficulty, to become acquainted together with the same people, to be objects of the same hospitality and kindness."
>
> Jane Griffin to John Franklin, summer 1828

Franklin's return from his second expedition cemented his reputation. As in the first case, he was showered with recognition: a gold medal from the French Geographical Society, a knighthood, and an honorary degree from Oxford. He also found a new wife.

In November 1828, when he had been back for fourteen months, Franklin married Jane Griffin. He had met her through Eleanor and had spent a considerable time in her company before the second expedition. As his first wife sickened, Franklin was not above socializing on his own. He dined at the Griffin home on a Sunday, a day he usually reserved for religion and family. He escorted Jane and her sister Fanny to dances and parties, and the sisters took a carriage down to Woolwich docks where Franklin was preparing boats for the expedition. None of this indicates that Franklin was being unfaithful, for Eleanor too was very fond of the Griffins. On one occasion when she felt up to entertaining, she invited them round to dine and meet Franklin's fellow explorer Captain Parry. However, when Franklin was with the Griffins he appears to have monopolized Jane's company. After a dinner party she recorded in her diary that Franklin had kept her in "continual conversation."

Franklin was obviously attracted to Jane. She was on his mind during his two-and-a-half-year-long second expedition, and he seems to have wasted no time in paying her court upon his return.

Jane Griffin and John Franklin were as well matched as John and Eleanor were not. Jane had a much more practical intelligence than her predecessor. She was witty, but not in Eleanor's somewhat strained, self-conscious way, and she was not averse to teasing her John. "Oh, what a coaxing smooth-tongued rogue you are," she wrote in reference to his description of a diplomatic incident he was involved in, "Who would think, my dear, that you had lived amongst the Polar bears?"

Jane had an independent mind and held strong opinions, some wrong, on a wide variety of topics. Some contemporaries felt this strength spilled over into arrogance, but Jane was fiercely loyal to Franklin, and it is mainly due to her strength of character and independence of mind that we know as much as we do about her husband's ultimate fate.

In the summer of 1828, John and Jane travelled to Russia. John wanted them to travel together but, since they were not yet married, convention demanded that they travel separately.

Since Franklin, on his second expedition, had mapped part of the coast of Alaska, which was then Russian territory, the visit was something of a diplomatic mission. Franklin met the Empress and the ten-year-old heir, the future Czar Alexander II. Through the boy's tutor, Franklin carefully described his journeys. It must have been a thrilling moment for the young prince, who already had an interest in geography and looked to the west as a model for the reforms he would introduce into his backward country before he was assassinated in 1881.

John and Jane spent their honeymoon in Paris, where Franklin was treated as a celebrity. People clamoured to meet him. One woman found the meeting a disappointing experience when she was eventually faced with an obviously healthy, ninety-five kilogram man. Her reading about Franklin's first expedition had led her to expect an emaciated skeleton.

Although he remained religious throughout his life, Franklin's puritan streak appears to have mellowed from the days of his arguments with Eleanor. While in Paris he visited all fifteen of the theatres. Given the reputation some Paris theatres had as places of ill-repute, this would have required a fairly broad mind.

Back in Britain, Franklin proposed further Arctic adventures to complete his mapping of the Canadian coastline. He was supported in this by Jane, who was extremely ambitious for her husband. She appears to have actively encouraged him to seek positions in the far-flung corners of the world. It seems odd that she should encourage him to desert her, but she explained it in a letter to him, "Your credit and reputation are dearer to me than the selfish enjoyment of your society. Nor indeed can I properly enjoy your society if you are living in inactivity when you might be in active employ."

Franklin, who had spent his whole life in active pursuits, was not the sort of person who takes kindly to inactivity. He had no literary or cultural pretensions and found living at home with nothing to do very hard. Jane recognized this need in her husband, and having a practical turn of mind, she realized that he, and consequently they, would only be happy if Franklin were actively employed.

Jane had confidence in Franklin's abilities and tended to underrate, as most people in the early nineteenth century did, the harshness of the Arctic climate and the inadequacy of the technology of the time to protect explorers from it in the event that something went wrong. In a hideously ironic contrast to the horrors of Franklin's final expedition, she wrote to him in late 1833, "a freezing climate seems to have a wonderful power in bracing your nerves and making you stronger."

In 1830, Franklin and his new wife had had two years of "vanity, trifling and idleness." For whatever reason, the Admiralty was ignoring Franklin's proposal to complete his Arctic mapping. However, they did eventually realize that they had an able officer wasting his talents and appointed him the command of the twenty-six gun frigate *Rainbow*. Two years and six days after his wedding, Franklin sailed for the Mediterranean.

Greece was newly independent from Turkey, and Britain, France, and Russia were in unusual agreement that this independence should be preserved. Unfortunately, rival factions were struggling for power, and the political instability this produced, combined with the scheming undertaken by the three major powers, required some very diplomatic maneuvering.

For two years, Franklin and the *Rainbow* cruised the Mediterranean, stopping in Malta, Nauplia, and Corfu, where Jane – Lady Jane Franklin since her husband's knighthood – came to spend some time with him. In 1832, Franklin sailed to Patras in southern Greece at the request of the local governor, who was anticipating an attack by a local rival.

The attack did not materialize, and the governor may have regretted asking for help when Franklin took the side of some Ionian merchants, British subjects at that time, who felt they were being unfairly taxed. Soldiers had been billeted with the merchants until their taxes were paid. Franklin's problem in this confrontation was that any action he took might spark a diplomatic incident. His only strength was the visible presence of the *Rainbow*'s twenty-six guns and her crew of trained sailors and marines. He probably could not have used them, but the governor could not be sure of that. Franklin insisted that the merchants be allowed to board the *Rainbow* for protection if they wished and arranged a meeting with the governor.

Franklin took a conciliatory tone, begging the governor to consider the consequences of not treating the merchants fairly and placing the heavy responsibility for what might happen on the governor's shoulders. Franklin did not state what the consequences might be – he left that to the governor's imagination – but the threat, veiled and dubious though it was, was there. By ignoring the governor's protests and consistently repeating his theme, Franklin won. The governor allowed the merchants to board the ship, and although he never withdrew his demands, the taxes were never collected.

Only a week later, Franklin faced a second delicate crisis. Easter in Patras was traditionally a time of wild celebration and it was often accompanied by much violence. In 1834, a General named Zavellas was suspected of planning to bring his troops in and plunder the city during the celebrations. The governor, his previous argument with Franklin apparently forgotten, requested troops to keep the peace.

Franklin's problem here was that he could not be seen to take sides in a local conflict in an independent country. Nevertheless, the situation appeared serious enough to intervene. A party of 140 British and French seamen went ashore. Franklin issued a proclamation that they had no political purpose and were there only to prevent disorder, and he requested the help of local soldiers and civilians. His ploy worked and Patras had one of its quietest Easters in a long time.

Franklin also had to deal with the intrigues of his allies. The Russians took to circling the British and French ships in rowboats in the dead of night. They carried no lights and refused to answer when hailed. Franklin suspected they were spying. He and the French captain wrote a note to the Russian commander. "We beg to be acquainted with the meaning of this unusual proceeding.... It is not our wish, Sir, to prevent your boats rowing about at night if you think it advisable, but we desire that they should not...present the appearance of watching our ships." Franklin also pointed out that the Russian boats, by not answering a hail, were putting themselves in danger of being fired upon.

The Russian commander replied that his boats were out in order to "protect" the allied vessels. However, he took the hint and after Franklin's note, his unorthodox protection was withdrawn.

In February 1833, the new king of Greece arrived and the *Rainbow* was sent home. Franklin had shown himself to be flexible and diplomatic in a very complex and tense situation. He seemed to be able to judge exactly how far he could go without committing himself to an action he might regret.

Franklin's time in the Mediterranean was also marked by his popularity amongst the sailors who served with him. His ship was called the "Celestial Rainbow" and "Franklin's Paradise" because of the relaxed atmosphere on board and the happy spirit. In an age when brutality was commonly regarded as necessary to control the criminal elements that were often on board Navy ships, Franklin was seen to tremble with emotion when he witnessed a man flogged. His gentle nature and subtle diplomacy are well recorded from this time in his career. On his return home he was commended on his "calm and steady conduct" and his "judgment and forbearance…exhibited under circumstances of repeated opposition and provocation."

Franklin left the *Rainbow* on January 8, 1834. He was forty-seven years old with over thirty years experience in almost all aspects of naval life. He was interviewed by the King, who thanked him and expressed great interest in tales of his exploits. Oddly, although Franklin's talents were widely recognized, he did not immediately receive a new posting. When Franklin went to see the First Lord of the Admiralty to ask for a posting, he was brushed off with the old, empty promise that he would be kept in mind should anything turn up.

Perhaps Franklin suffered from a lack of influential friends in high places, or perhaps he did not put himself forward forcefully enough. Certainly he admitted to being shy and timid and stated that he only tried as hard as he did because Jane wished him to do so.

It was not that there was no Arctic exploration going on. James and John Ross had been rescued in 1833 after spending four winters in the Arctic. During that time, James had discovered the North Magnetic

Pole and visited the north shore of King William Island, a place Franklin's crew would become horribly familiar with fifteen years later. Franklin's old companion, George Back, had travelled overland down the river that was to be named after him and visited the Arctic coast, although he had failed to map the area east of Point Turnagain.

In 1834, the government was considering another expedition to the Northwest Passage. The three great Arctic explorers of their day, Edward Parry, James Ross, and John Franklin were all available to lead it, but the choice fell again to Back. In June 1836 he sailed north in HMS *Terror*. The expedition was nearly a disaster and no new ground was discovered. Meanwhile, Franklin's career was taking a different turn on the other side of the world.

Franklin, possibly at the prompting of Jane, was, in 1836, considering a position in the colonies. He submitted his name and qualifications to the Colonial Office and was offered the post of governor of the tiny West Indian island of Antigua. This remote posting was a powerless one under the governor-in-chief of the Leeward Islands. Jane thought it unworthy of her husband and encouraged him to turn it down. Franklin did so, and his stand appears to have impressed the Colonial Office. Less that two weeks after his refusal, Franklin was offered the much larger and more prestigious Van Diemen's Land (Tasmania) at a salary of £2,500 per annum. He accepted and sailed for his new posting later that year. There would follow six years which would sorely test all the qualities of perseverance and discretion he had shown in the Mediterranean.

National Library of Australia, PIC U66. Artist: Charles Hutchins.

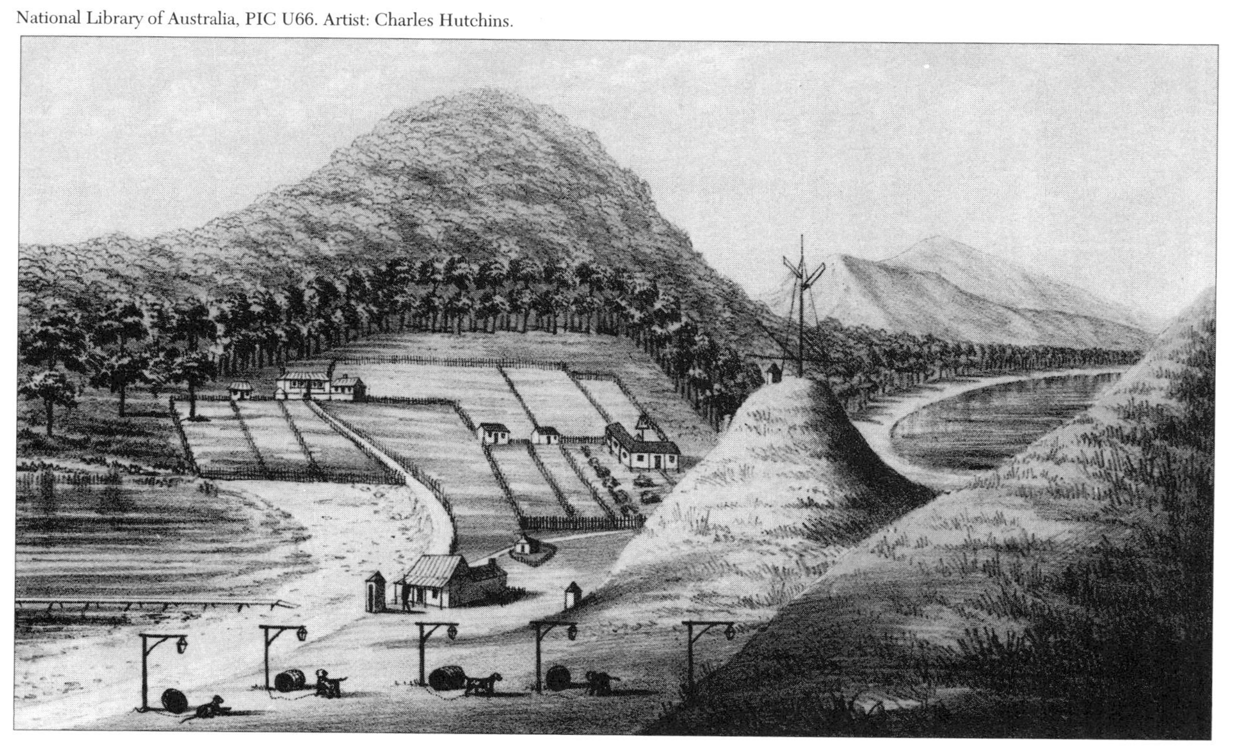

To escape, you first had to pass the line of vicious dogs. Eagle Hawk Neck, Van Diemen's Land.

10

Van Diemen's Land

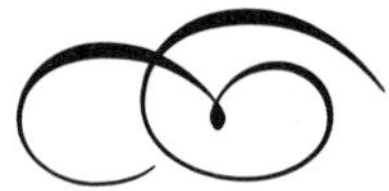

The very day we landed
    upon the fatal shore,
The planters they stood round us
    full twenty score or more;
They ranked us up like horses
    and sold us out of hand,
They roped us to the plough, brave boys,
    to plough Van Diemen's Land.

Convict Ballad

In the 1820s, a line of convict loggers was walking through the bush to work near the penal settlement at Macquarie Harbour on the west coast of Van Diemen's Land. Without warning or provocation, one man in the middle of the line suddenly raised his axe and smashed it down on the head of the man ahead of him. He made no attempt to escape and was arrested. When asked why he had killed a man against whom he had no grudge, the killer stated simply that he had run out of tobacco. He knew that if he was to be hanged for murder it would be in Hobart and he would be given tobacco in the jail there. Such was the brutal irrationality bred in the convict hell of Van Diemen's Land.

Van Diemen's Land was a new colony, not even in existence when Franklin had passed that way with Flinders. Of the 42,000 European population when Franklin took over as governor, almost half were convicts transported there for a variety of crimes from petty theft to murder. Between 1831 and 1835, 133 vessels had brought 26,731 convicts to Australia, many to Van Diemen's Land. Transport conditions had improved markedly after the Napoleonic Wars ended and the threat of starvation faced by the early colonists had faded, but often that merely meant that the individual lived longer in abject misery.

In Van Diemen's Land, the convicts were not held in prison, but were scattered through the community on assignment as employees of the free settlers. Assignment provided the essential labour for the free farmers, but it was little more than slavery, and the prisoner was at the complete mercy of the settler. Franklin's predecessor, George Arthur, even introduced rules forbidding the settlers to fraternize with, or even show kindness to, their assigned men and women. One settler lost his assignment privileges for inviting his labourers to sit down with his family for Christmas dinner.

Life was harsh and punishment brutal. For even minor offenses, convicts were flogged, forced to work in chains, or placed in solitary confinement. The hardness of life made the people – convicts and free settlers alike – hard too. Gambling, drinking, and theft were all prevalent. Escaped convicts roamed the bush, hunting, or robbing travellers and isolated farms. But by far the greatest sufferers as a result of the settlement of Van Diemen's Land were the native inhabitants.

There were, perhaps, three to four thousand Aborigines in Van Diemen's Land when the first ships arrived. They had lived there for thirty thousand years. The convicts and first settlers regarded the indigenous inhabitants as animals. They saw no problem in deliberately poisoning, spreading disease, or resettling the Aborigines. They even hunted them for sport. By Franklin's day, the Aboriginal population had been reduced to a mere 150 people, living in squalor on Flinders Island in Bass Strait. In 1876, Trucanini, the last Tasmanian Aborigine, died. Her death marked the end of the only case of true genocide in British history. Remembering the fate of her husband, whose body had been dismembered and distributed to scientific institutes, Trucanini's last words were, "Don't let them cut me, but bury me behind the mountains." No one listened. Trucanini's flesh was boiled off her bones and her skeleton exhibited in the Tasmanian Museum and Art Gallery. One hundred years later, in 1976, her bones were cremated and the ashes scattered at sea.

ꟹ

When Franklin stepped ashore with his family in January 1837, he took over a colony that had been run with an iron fist. Governor Arthur had seen his domain as a vast experiment in social engineering, on a smaller scale, but well in advance of the experiments of Hitler and Stalin. He had created a totalitarian state, with every aspect of the convicts' and settlers' lives catalogued and recorded. In 1826 he had drawn up the three-feet-thick, "Black Books" in which were recorded every detail of the lives of every one of the 12,305 convicts who had arrived since the colony's founding. On arrival, convicts were interrogated to ensure that the books were kept up to date. Van Diemen's Land had the most complete record of its inhabitants of any place on earth.

A prisoner was subject to seven levels of punishment between the extremes of freedom and hanging. He rose or fell through the levels depending upon his conduct. One historian has likened it to a vast game of human Snakes and Ladders.

The system was brutal, but the evangelical Arthur's aim, however misguided, was to reform the convicts. It didn't work and only increased the brutalizing effects of the harsh life in the colony. To console himself, Arthur used his power as governor to acquire a fortune. He left Van Diemen's Land a rich man, was made lieutenant-governor of Upper Canada in 1838 after William Lyon MacKenzie's rebellion, and was knighted for his role in uniting Upper and Lower Canada in 1841.

Arthur was roundly detested by most of the free settlers who welcomed Franklin. Unfortunately, the system Franklin inherited was run by Arthur's men, several of whose only qualifications were that they were intelligent enough to have married one of Arthur's relatives. Yet Franklin had to rely on them for what the Colonial Office back in Britain saw as the smooth running of the colony. After all, Van Diemen's Land was meant to be a convict settlement, not an earthly paradise, and the idea of prisoners' rights was virtually unknown. The settlers soon developed a healthy dislike for Franklin. This was exacerbated by a strong dislike of Jane.

Jane Franklin was strong-willed, intelligent, curious, and restless. The settlers interpreted these characteristics as bossy, pretentious, nosy, and interfering. She certainly felt she should have a role in the colony. Influenced by Elizabeth Fry, who was working for prison reform in Britain, Jane formed the "Tasmanian Ladies' Society for the Reformation of Female Prisoners." It was not welcomed and was short-lived.

In emulation of St. Patrick in Ireland, Jane also tried to rid Van Diemen's Land of snakes. Prisoners were offered a shilling for each dead snake. Unfortunately, since there were a lot more snakes on the island than there were shillings in the governor's budget, the scheme failed.

Jane had more luck encouraging the arts. She supported learned societies, established a botanical garden and museum of Natural History, and founded a college. She was also an avid traveller, being the first woman to travel overland from Melbourne to Sydney, to ascend Mount Wellington, and to travel overland from Hobart to Macquarie Harbour. In the parochial, uncultured society of Hobart, none of this carried any weight, and Jane was detested for what was perceived as gross interference in her husband's affairs. Her husband was also condemned for allowing her so much apparent power.

Franklin's gentleness was not an advantage in Van Diemen's Land. Jane wrote that to live in the colony, "people should have hearts of stone and frames of steel." Franklin, the man who had trembled when he witnessed a sailor flogged aboard ship, did not have a heart of stone. In addition, he was politically naive, even timid according to some sources. In the dog-eat-dog world of isolated colonial politics and infighting, Franklin was out of his depth. He could be astute politically, as he had proved on his Mediterranean posting, but there he had been in charge of a rigid naval structure that had obeyed him unquestioningly. In Van Diemen's Land he was powerless amidst opposing factions who felt no loyalty other than to their own narrow interests and who would use any means to achieve their ends. The local press was their vehicle. Almost every edition of the Hobart papers contained something which, if published today, would land its author in court for libel. In the broad journey of Franklin's life, the six years in Van Diemen's Land were not a happy experience. However, Franklin did manage brief journeys that were more to his liking.

After four years of difficult and disagreeable life in Hobart, Franklin was given a sharp reminder of his previous life and, perhaps, a pang of regret at the glimpse of what might have been his had he not become stuck in this unpleasant place.

In 1839, James Ross had sailed south from London. He had two ships, the *Erebus* and the *Terror*, and orders to explore and circumnavigate the little-known Antarctic Continent. His second-in-command, captain of the *Terror*, and in charge of the important magnetic work, was also an old Arctic hand, the Irishman, Francis Rawdon Moira Crozier.

In August 1840, the expedition arrived in Hobart. Franklin was overjoyed. He invited Ross and Crozier to stay at Government House. Ross was charged with examining magnetism as close to the South Pole as possible. Franklin supplied convict labour to build Ross's magnetic observatory on a hill outside Hobart. He attended a ball Ross threw in his honour on board the *Erebus*, and when Ross briefly returned to Hobart in 1841, Franklin went out aboard his barge to meet the ships as soon as they were sighted. His spirits picked up and the colonists saw a different side of their governor. Jane described him as, "bustling and frisky and merry with his new companions."

Looking at his portraits, it is a little difficult to imagine Franklin as "frisky," but he was certainly in good spirits. To have the company of people with the same interests and a broad view of the world was gratifying. There was even a romantic interlude played out in the drawing rooms of Government House. Sophia Cracroft, daughter of Franklin's favourite sister,

Isabella, and companion to Jane, fell head-over-heels in love with James Ross. Ross however, remained faithful to his fiancee back in England. To complicate the situation, Crozier fell for Sophia, to the degree that he actually proposed marriage to her. She turned him down.

Franklin watched sadly as Ross sailed away. Had he stayed in Britain, could that have been him leading the expedition? He yearned to sit where Ross was, in the Great Cabin of the *Erebus*. Ironically, he would get his chance in a few years' time.

Meanwhile, although Franklin was stuck in this impossible and thankless job, governing the unruly population of Van Diemen's Land, perhaps there was something active he could do? There was – he could go exploring. Large tracts of Van Diemen's Land were unknown, and there was a need to open up more land for the increasing population of settlers and convicts. Franklin decided to examine the harsh landscape between Hobart and Macquarie Harbour.

In late March of 1842 he set out, accompanied by Jane, five settlers, and twenty convicts. The schooner *Breeze* would meet them at the mouth of the Gordon River. Almost as soon as they left Hobart, the weather turned nasty. Buffeted by storms, delayed by swollen streams, and increasingly wet and miserable, the party struggled on through the almost impenetrable wilderness. On one occasion, they camped at the foot of a mountain, on the only piece of solid ground around. The rain was so violent that they could not leave their tiny island of dry security for a week. Food began to run low and Franklin introduced rationing. With his sense of fairness, Franklin insisted that the larger rations be given to the convicts who were doing all the work.

Eventually, the struggling party came to halt at a river in flood. To Franklin it was a echo of the horrible delay on the Coppermine River twenty years before. The *Breeze* was due to sail in two days. She wouldn't wait, and if Franklin's party couldn't reach her before she sailed, they would starve. Two convicts volunteered to cross the river on a makeshift raft. The violent, swirling waters swept them downstream through some rapids, but they gained the other bank and reached the *Breeze* just as she was setting sail. They persuaded the ship's Captain to wait until Franklin's slower party crossed the river and joined them. It appeared as if Franklin had been saved in the nick of time once more, but the expedition's trials were not over. Storms prevented the *Breeze* from sailing, and the spectre of starvation raised its head again.

When at last the storms abated, Franklin returned to Hobart to discover that the entire party was assumed dead. He was discouraged to find that, even in death he was given no leeway by the hostile press. "Pity is out of the question," was the comment of one local newspaper.

Franklin's explorations in Van Diemen's Land threatened him with starvation and left him at the mercy of the elements. It was an unpleasant experience, yet Franklin remembered it as one of the few times he was happy. To Franklin the man of action, starving or freezing to death appeared preferable to the political infighting of governing the colony.

Franklin was unlucky in Van Diemen's Land. Through no fault of his own, the economy was in a slump and his tenure happened to coincide with a change of policy by the British government that threatened the settlers' beloved assignment system. Nevertheless, his main problem was his own Colonial Secretary, the ex-Arthur man, John Montagu. Montagu was intelligent but conniving, insidious, and totally unscrupulous. Franklin's right-hand man was a part owner of one of the local papers into which he poured insults and innuendo aimed at discrediting his boss and his wife. Such was the nature of politics in Van Diemen's Land.

Franklin allowed Montagu to carry on this way for years. Perhaps Franklin believed the man capable of reform. If so he was seriously mistaken. Despite obvious kindness towards him on Franklin's part, Montagu kept up his attacks relentlessly, even going to Britain for two years to spread poisonous lies behind the governor's back. Eventually, he went too far even for Franklin's tolerance. In reply to a memorandum from Franklin, Montagu responded insultingly that while his own memory was "remarkably accurate," even Franklin's officers had learned that they "could not always place implicit confidence" in their superior's memory. Montagu often implied Franklin was feeble-minded, but now he had put it in writing. This was Franklin's opportunity. He suspended Montagu and wrote explaining his case to the Secretary for the Colonies in London.

Montagu hastened back to Britain to defend himself. There he was presented with an extraordinary piece of luck. The new Secretary for the Colonies was Lord Stanley, who would become famous for being Prime Minister three times without managing to accomplish anything of any note whatsoever. Incredibly, Stanley believed every word Montagu told him, entirely discounted Franklin's letter, and refused even to give his own governor an opportunity to defend himself.

Stanley wrote a dispatch to Franklin defending Montagu. He then gave a copy to Montagu and delayed sending the original to Franklin. Thus, the contents of the dispatch were well known in Hobart gossip circles before Franklin heard of them. Franklin responded to Stanley, remarkably mildly given the circumstances, and was rewarded by being immediately recalled.

The recall lifted a burden from Franklin's shoulders. His spirits improved and he ironically wished his successor joy in "what he has in store for him." Even the local populace appeared to have a change of heart, and a large cheering crowd turned out to see the Franklins off.

The years in Van Diemen's Land were both a trial and a career disaster for Franklin. He did not do anything wrong and was poorly served both by his subordinates and his superiors; nevertheless, he failed in the brutal arena of colonial politics. It was unlikely he would be given another posting of any significance.

When Franklin returned to Britain in 1844, he was fifty-eight years old. He had not led an expedition for seventeen years, yet he still regarded himself as an explorer. He could have retired comfortably and been regarded as a competent man of his time who had filled in useful pieces of the map of the Canadian Arctic. But Franklin felt he had missed opportunities for true greatness. As it turned out, fate was to give him one more chance. He failed again. This time it was a failure of such monumental proportions that John Franklin's fame would eclipse that of his contemporaries and secure him a place in our cultural memory achieved by very few.

11

King William Island

> 25th April 1848 HM Ships *Terror* and *Erebus* were deserted on the 22nd April 5 leagues NNW of this having been beset since 12th Sept. 1846. The Officers & Crews consisting of 105 souls under the command of Captain F.R.M. Crozier landed here.... Sir John Franklin died on the 11th June 1847 and the total loss by deaths in the Expedition has been to this date 9 officers & 15 men.
>
> Last message from Franklin's doomed expedition

On April 25, 1848, three British naval officers sat composing the above message in a windblown tent on the ice-covered shores of King William Island,

National Library of Australia T398. Artist: Edward William Cooke.

Before the ice finally trapped them. The ill-fated *Erebus* and *Terror* at sea.

one of the most remote and bleakest places on earth. They had accomplished much, mapped new lands, described new animals and plants, and filled in the last one hundred kilometres of the fabled Northwest Passage. But they were close to the end. They had been in the Canadian Arctic for three years. Their vessels were still intact, but the fearful pack ice had not released them the previous summer. They still had food left, but men were dying at an alarming rate. Scurvy, the dread of all exploring parties, was widespread. They were more than a thousand kilometres from the closest help. They were doomed. They would keep on struggling to survive, some for perhaps another two years, but none of the three officers or their 102 companions would ever see home again.

Back on May 19, 1845, the day they sailed from England, it was overcast, but there was a festive mood in the air as the ships cast off from the Greenhithe dock at 10:30 that morning. For many it was an adventure they greeted with almost schoolboy enthusiasm. They expected to be gone only a year, and some even hoped for a minor delay so that they could spend more time in the mysterious Arctic. An added bonus was that, like all men on "Exploration Service," they would collect double pay as long as they were at sea. As the ships cast off that May morning, a dove alighted on the masthead of one. Surely this was an omen of good fortune.

How could an expedition which began with such unbridled optimism have gone so wrong? The officers in the tent didn't know, and people are still arguing about it today, but the three men probably agreed that the turning point had been June 11 of the previous year – the day their commander, Sir John Franklin, died.

John Franklin was not the first choice to command the new Arctic venture. The first choice had been James Ross, who had just returned from his circumnavigation of the Antarctic continent. But Ross was a new husband and father, and his young bride, with an attitude starkly in contrast to that of Jane Franklin, had asked him to remain at home and not to undertake any more long and dangerous voyages.

Sir John Barrow, who had been the driving force behind almost every Arctic expedition since Franklin first went north with Buchan in 1818, favoured James Fitzjames, a rising young star in the Royal Navy who had seen service in the Middle East and China. But Fitzjames had never been to the Arctic and lacked experience in ice navigation.

So, at the third go around, the choice fell to Franklin. He had all the qualifications except one. He was old. Almost fifty-nine is old to undergo the rigours of nineteenth-century Arctic travel, but who else was there? And Franklin was keen. Edward Parry was asked if he thought Franklin should be given command. He replied: "He is a fitter man to go than any I know, and if you don't let him go, the man will die of disappointment."

The selection of second-in-command was no easier. Again Barrow wanted Fitzjames, but the post was offered to a Captain Stokes. When Stokes declined, it was given to Francis Crozier, Ross's second-in-command in the Antarctic and the would-be suitor to Sophia Cracroft.

Crozier should have been an obvious choice for leader of the expedition. He had more ice navigation experience than any of the others and had proven himself reliable and thorough on innumerable occasions. He was also only forty-eight, but he had one huge handicap: He was not socially acceptable. He was Irish and Protestant, and not a member of the elite English aristocratic club. Thus he was suited for work but not command. With Crozier as second-in-command, Fitzjames was finally taken on as third-in-command.

Although the expedition was organized on short notice, no expense was spared. Ross's ships, the *Erebus* and *Terror*, were specially strengthened and had steam engines added for navigation in ice. The ships were supplied with desalinators to distill fresh water from seawater and a steam heating system. Food for three years included 61,986 kilograms of flour, 29,132 kilograms of salt beef and pork, 4,286 kilograms of chocolate, 16,747 litres of concentrated spirits, 4,218 kilograms of lemon juice, 91 kilograms of pepper, and almost 8,000 cans of meat. The ships' libraries contained 2,900 books, including technical manuals, the reports of previous explorers, and the works of Dickens. The infant art of photography was represented by an early daguerreotype apparatus, and each ship was equipped with a hand-organ capable of playing fifty different tunes. This was the ultimate expression of Franklin's idea that you should take everything with you. The 129 men who sailed into Lancaster Sound aboard the *Erebus* and *Terror* would live as closely as possible to the way they did at home, at least until things began to go wrong.

Franklin's orders were to proceed through Lancaster Sound and Barrow Strait until he reached Cape Walker. Since Parry had found massive amounts of permanent ice to the west, Franklin was told to sail south and west towards the Canadian Arctic coast. He was to take the straightest line he could, given that the huge area on the map was unknown and probably contained as yet undiscovered land. If he found the southern route blocked, he was to try sailing to the north along Wellington Channel in another attempt to find the supposed open Arctic Ocean that had proved elusive in 1818.

On the way, Franklin and his officers were charged with taking magnetic, oceanographic, and meteorological readings, sampling the geology, and examining everything, "from a flea to a whale." They would sail the Northwest Passage, but they were primarily a scientific expedition.

In keeping with the spirit of scientific innovation, Jane Franklin commissioned two sets of daguerreotype portraits of the officers on the *Erebus*. The daguerreotype process, a precursor of the negative photography of today, was only six years old. It required over forty kilograms of equipment to fix an image on a silvered metal plate. It also required the subject to remain immobile for several minutes. This, as much as the formality of the day, accounts for the rigid poses of the officers when they sat in the Great Cabin of the *Erebus* for Mr. Beard, the only licensed daguerreotype practitioner in Britain.

Daguerreotype plates last extraordinarily well and are as sharp today as when they were exposed. The originals, archived in Britain, have an almost ethereal silvery patina, which imparts a magical, poignant feel, considering what we know of the fate of these men. To a modern observer, only Fitzjames and Franklin look at all natural. For his second daguerreotype, Commander Fitzjames discarded his telescope prop and smiled faintly for posterity.

In both of his portraits, although he is dressed in his formal uniform, is wearing his impressive medals, and is carrying his gold baton, Sir John Franklin looks as if he would much rather be somewhere else. Two of his uniform buttons are undone, his face looks pasty, and his eyes puffy. That day, he had a bad case of the flu. He felt horribly unwell, but he had also just had an unnerving premonition.

A couple of nights before the portraits were taken, Franklin was sitting at home by the fire with Jane. He was resting and trying to throw off the flu. She was busy making a silk Union Jack flag for her husband to take with him and raise at the completion of the Northwest Passage. John dropped off to sleep on the couch and, fearing he might be cold, Jane draped the unfinished flag over him. Franklin, the lifetime navy man, awoke to find himself covered in the flag. Jumping up in horror, he said, "There's a flag thrown over me! Don't you know that they lay a Union Jack over a corpse?"

It took Franklin some time to recover his composure, but recover he did, and the *Erebus* and *Terror* set off for their first stop at Stromness in the Orkney

Islands, north of the Scottish mainland. Expectations ran universally high. Sir Roderick Murchison, President of the Royal Geographical Society, stated: "I have the fullest confidence that everything will be done..., that human efforts can accomplish. The name of Franklin alone is, indeed, a national guarantee." The *Times* newspaper of London voiced what it perceived as the, "one wish amongst the whole of the inhabitants of this country, from the humblest individual to the highest in the realm, that the enterprise...may be attended with success, and that the brave seamen...may return with honour and health to their native land."

After a stormy Atlantic crossing, on July 4 Franklin arrived off the island of Disco on the west coast of Greenland and began transferring supplies to his two ships. The process took six days. Before the *Erebus* and *Terror* sailed on the tide on July 12, five of the luckiest men in Arctic exploration history were sent home for illness or incompetence, and everyone took the opportunity to write letters to loved ones in Britain. In them, the officers talk of Franklin's energy, enthusiasm, and leadership.

Setting off exploring once more gave John Franklin a new lease on life. Once he had recovered from his cold, he looked ten years younger and took a great interest in all the voyage's activities. He regularly dined with his officers, regaling them with tales of his previous exploits, and conducted religious services every Sunday. The young men under his command almost worshipped him. They were in awe of his experience and judgment and treasured his friendship: "We are very happy, and very fond of Sir John Franklin, who improves very much as we come to know more of him. He is anything but nervous and fidgety: in fact, I should say remarkable for energetic decision in sudden emergencies." The *Erebus* was a new "Franklin's Paradise."

Franklin himself was happier than he had been in years. At last he was back doing what he loved most; leading a party of energetic and zealous subordinates into the unknown. He wrote to all his friends back in England to make sure they would "comfort and assist" Jane in his absence. He even petitioned God in his "constant prayers" to "bless and support" her. They were the last words she ever received from him.

When nothing was heard of Franklin for three years, people began to be concerned, and one of the largest search operations in history slowly got under way. Over the next decade, thirty-two expeditions went to the Arctic seeking to discover what had happened to John Franklin. In doing so, they mapped vastly more territory than Franklin could ever have hoped to do on his own and joined the Arctic to the map of Canada. But they found precious little hard evidence of Franklin's fate.

It wasn't until 1850 that Franklin's first wintering site was discovered at Beechey Island. Here were the remains of buildings, piles of empty food cans, and three graves, but no message to say which way the expedition had gone. The searchers fanned out but discovered nothing else.

In 1854 John Rae of the Hudson's Bay Company returned to England with some relics and a story to tell. The relics, which had been obtained from the Inuit, included the medal Franklin was wearing in the daguerreotype and some officer's cutlery, but it was the Inuit stories that captured the public's attention. They told of abandoned boats, starving men, and, least acceptable to Victorian sensibilities, cannibalism. Rae was shouted down by such notables as Charles Dickens for believing the unsubstantiated ramblings of untutored savages, but it was enough evidence for the Royal Navy. They declared Franklin and all his men dead and stopped their double pay.

But the stories were not enough for the indomitable Jane Franklin. She wanted to know what had happened to the husband she had encouraged to go exploring. She badgered the navy mercilessly and, when that didn't produce the results she wanted, she financed her own expedition. It was led by Francis Leopold McClintock and, in 1859, fourteen years after Franklin had sailed with such high hopes, a sledging party from McClintock's yacht, the *Fox*, arrived at Victory Point on King William Island. There they found piles of clothing and supplies and a solitary note, sealed in a tin can and buried beneath a cairn of stones. Along the coast they also found an abandoned ship's boat and the scattered bones of Franklin's men.

In the years since, more bones have been discovered and new scientific techniques have been used to explain what happened. The disaster has been blamed on murder, starvation, scurvy, bad food, lead poisoning, and, most recently, botulism poisoning. Some of the theories are wild, and most tell us more about our own fears than they do about Franklin, but it is now possible to piece together a rough outline of what happened.

Franklin led his happy band of explorers through Lancaster Sound in August, 1845. Not being one to disobey orders, he sailed straight on to Cape Walker and tried to turn south. There he met the Beaufort Ice Stream, pouring down from the High Arctic. It was a fearful sight of vast slabs of ice grinding and crashing together – there was no way through. Retreating, Franklin tried the second option in his orders, a northern route. He sailed up Wellington Channel and reached 77 degrees north before ice again stopped him. He returned south, circumnavigated Cornwallis Island, and settled in for the winter at the protected bay beside Beechey Island.

The first winter still felt like an adventure. The men occupied themselves with the scientific work, explored the coastline, and hunted. They built a forge and storage hut on the shore and even attempted to plant a garden in the spring. Three men died – too many deaths in such a short time – but all three had been suffering from consumption, the same disease that had killed Franklin's first wife. The sick men should never have been in the Arctic in the first place. Everyone else was fit and well.

In the summer of 1846, the ice broke up and Franklin had a piece of good luck. He discovered an open channel to the south down the side of Somerset Island. He could carry out his orders after all.

Hurrying on in the short summer season, the *Erebus* and *Terror* used their steam engines in close ice to work down to a position north of King William Island. James Ross had visited King William Island in 1830, and this was the farthest anyone had gone through the Northwest Passage from the east. A mere one hundred kilometres to the south was the cairn built by two Hudson's Bay Company men – Thomas Simpson and the very same Peter Warren Dease who had been such a help organizing Franklin's supplies on his second expedition. Only eight years before, they had mapped the coast along from Franklin's Point Turnagain and visited the south shore of King William Island. Franklin was poised to complete the Northwest Passage.

Perhaps Franklin tried to pass down the east coast of King William Island, but it is too shallow there for the deep drafts of his ships, so he would have had to turn back. The only other choice was the west coast. This was not an inviting prospect, for down there ran the extension of the frightening Beaufort Ice Stream. There were no protected harbours on the west coast, so Franklin had to make the best of it, docking his ships for the winter in a stable ice floe in the stream. It was not ideal, but still nothing to worry about. Another winter and the Northwest Passage would be theirs. Then they could sail home along the coast of Canada and return as heroes.

In the spring of 1847, still full of hope, Franklin sent out a sledging expedition to examine the west coast of King William Island and complete the Northwest Passage. Lieutenant Graham Gore from the *Erebus* succeeded, and for his achievement was promoted by Franklin to Commander. Gore left brief notes in cairns to mark his progress along the coast. As Gore's commander it was Fitzjames' duty to write the notes, which were all written before Gore set off and which all ended with the cheery "All well." It was the last time anyone could say that.

On June 11, 1847, John Franklin died. It was unexpected. He had been fine when Fitzjames wrote "All well" on the 24th of May. Perhaps it was a heart attack or a stroke. Franklin was now sixty-one and, despite the expedition's good progress so far, Arctic exploration was a hard discipline for a man that age. In any case, his death was a severe blow to morale. Franklin was the leader, the figurehead, and his name was, after all, the "national guarantee."

Did Franklin have any warning of his end? Did he have a chance to write one last letter to Jane, his other half and the one person who had always believed in and supported him? No one knows. If he did, it was lost with all the rest of the expedition's papers.

Crozier was now in charge. His first duty was to bury Franklin, either in the ice or at some undiscovered place on King William Island. It must have been a very emotional occasion. Franklin had been almost like a father to many of the young, inexperienced officers on the *Erebus*, and without him, the whole tone of the expedition changed. Crozier was an efficient, practical man and he would do his best, but he did not have Franklin's presence. The men knew that even when the ice released them in the summer of 1847, they would sail home with a dark burden.

With Franklin's death, the expedition's good luck seemed to evaporate. The expected spring breakup of the ice didn't happen. The crews waited, keeping watch from the crow's-nest for the telltale glimpse of an open water lead, but nothing showed. All that happened was that the trapped ships drifted slowly to the south, ever deeper into the ice stream.

Soon they were facing another winter with no guarantee that the summer of 1848 would be any better. Men began dying of scurvy. Lead poisoning from the poorly soldered canned food began to set in. This was a mysterious illness because lead was not known as a poison in the 1840s.

In the spring of 1848, Crozier made a desperate decision. His ships were still undamaged, but he had to find fresh food to stop the scurvy. Other explorers had talked of caribou and birds to the south. After taking their equipment and supplies ashore, Crozier had Lieutenant John Irving retrieve one of Gore's messages. In the windblown tent, while Fitzjames wrote and Irving corrected, Crozier dictated the expedition's last message around the margins of the earlier one. Gore's cheery "All well" appeared horribly ironic now.

After they reburied the message, they headed south. Some men died on the way, dropping in their tracks; others died at a large camp on the south shore of King William Island; some made it onto the

Canadian mainland and died beneath an upturned boat at Starvation Cove; a dozen or so died beside a boat on the way back to the ships. A few made it back to the ships and probably sailed one of them south. But scurvy, lead poisoning, starvation, and ice would not let them succeed. These men all died too.

The Inuit tell stories of meeting ragged groups of starving men, of finding camps filled with bodies and the evidence of cannibalism, and, most intriguingly, of three or four men and a dog who survived for several years and reached as far east as the Melville Peninsula. But eventually they too died. Everyone died – often very unpleasantly and after witnessing and living through almost unspeakable horrors. Franklin's final piece of luck was that he did not live to see the tragedy that his final expedition became.

Photo by John Wilson.

Journeying after death. Memorial to John Franklin, Waterloo Place, London.

Epilogue

Westminster Abbey

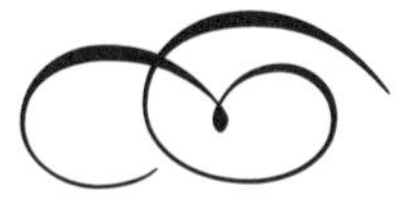

Not here:
The white North has thy bones, and thou
Heroic Sailor Soul
Art passing on thy happier voyage now
Toward no Earthly Pole.

Tennyson's epitaph to Franklin,
Westminster Abbey

The young Lieutenant Irving was one of those who returned to the ships in the summer of 1848. We know this because he was alive at Victory Point when the note was written in April and Crozier led his command south. In the 1870s, a skeleton in a shallow grave was found at Victory Point. Shreds of clothing indicated that it belonged to an officer. Beside the skull was a medal for mathematical achievement from the Royal Naval College, Portsmouth. It had been presented in 1830 to John Irving. Even in their last extremity, the survivors took the trouble to bury their friends surrounded by their most prized possessions.

Irving's skeleton was returned to Britain and, amidst widespread grief, was buried in his hometown of Edinburgh. His is the only named grave of any of the 129 men of the Franklin expedition.

Despite Jane's best efforts, John Franklin's grave was never found. However, monuments to him sprang up all around the world. A statue of Franklin announcing the discovery of the Northwest Passage to his men stands to one side of Waterloo Place in London. The statue is 2.4 metres high, and the plinth on which it stands bears a bronze scene of Franklin's funeral, a map, lists of all the officers and men of the *Erebus* and *Terror*, and the scars of a German bomb that exploded in Waterloo Place during the blitz in 1940. A marble monument in Westminster Abbey was unveiled by George Back in 1875, mere weeks after Jane Franklin died. There is a bas-relief in Greenwich, a statue, apparently a very good likeness, in the Market Place of Spilsby, stained glass windows in Gravesend, a monument in Hobart, Tasmania, and a marble tablet on Beechey Island. In addition, many points in the Canadian Arctic are named for Franklin and his companions.

John Franklin was gentler and less arrogant than many of his contemporaries, but his cultural blinkers were just as firmly in place. In structured environments where there was a clear chain of command, he excelled. In situations where the structure was fluid and flexibility and imagination were called for, he did less well. Yet he spent much of his life actively seeking those very situations.

Why he should have sought out dangerous, unstable situations, in which it was extremely unlikely that he would excel, is a mystery. Perhaps he had a distorted view of his own talents. Perhaps he saw his own weaknesses and attempted to overcome them. If the latter, then he failed.

Most likely, Franklin did not really question his situations. The early nineteenth century was not, after all, a time of great self-analysis. Franklin did what he did at each moment of his life because, at that time, there were obvious reasons for taking a specific course. He undertook exploration because Flinders had trained him well in navigation and because it was the fastest way to advance his career. He pushed the limits too far on his first expedition because not to have done so would have finished his career. He eagerly sought leadership of his third expedition because he longed for the straightforward life of an explorer after the years of political infighting in Van Diemen's Land.

But for all that, there was a part of Franklin that craved the solitude and hardship of remote places on the edge of the known world. To satisfy that craving he was perfectly prepared to risk his own and his companions' lives.

Maybe Franklin would have been better off staying at home and taking over the family business in Spilsby. But that was never really possible. John was a traveller. Two of his brothers sought their fortunes in India, but even India would not have been enough for John. He went to extremes. Few ventured as far as he did both in the far north and the far south. He pushed the limits of the known.

Franklin achieved much during his life. His expeditions mapped more than 12,735 kilometres of previously unknown coastline; his scientific discoveries contributed a great deal to an understanding of the ecology of the Arctic lands; and his men discovered the final link in the Northwest Passage.

Ironically, however, Franklin's greatest contribution to exploration and geography was his mysterious death. The navy had no shortage of keen young officers who could have led Franklin's first two expeditions as well as he. What was unique to Franklin was his death off the shores of King William Island. That event and attempts to explain it triggered one of the largest and most intense bursts of exploration the world has ever seen. What happened in the twelve years after Franklin died defined the Canadian North and set the scene for the sovereignty we now enjoy.

The North has always loomed large in the Canadian consciousness, and Franklin's tragic death has assumed the aura of a Canadian myth. The countless songs, stories, and poems written about him have extended his journey long past his own lifetime. Rudy Wiebe won the Governor General's Award for *A Discovery of Strangers*, his novel set around Franklin's first expedition. Stan Rogers' song, *Northwest Passage*, with its haunting images of "lonely cairns of stones" and "the hand of Franklin reaching for the Beaufort

Sea," was considered the ultimate Canadian song by CBC listeners.

We owe John Franklin a lot. He was a man of his time who failed to rise above that. He failed as much as he succeeded, but his final failure was so magnificent that it ensured him a lasting place in the history of Canada and in the minds of all Canadians.

Toronto Reference Library 919.8 B47BR.

Finding Remains of Skeletons in a Boat. Reprinted from E.V Blake, *Arctic Experiences* (1874). Two of Franklin's men after they became part of the myth.

Chronology of John Franklin (1786-1847)

Compiled by Lynne Bowen

FRANKLIN AND HIS TIMES

CANADA AND THE WORLD

1576
English explorer Martin Frobisher leads an unsuccessful expedition in search of the fabled Northwest Passage.

1580
English explorer Francis Drake embarks on a voyage around the world; one of his goals is to find the western end of the Northwest Passage.

1610-11
English explorer Henry Hudson, while searching for the Northwest Passage, sails into Hudson Bay; the crew mutinies and sets Hudson, his son and seven others adrift in an open boat; they are never seen again.

FRANKLIN AND HIS TIMES	CANADA AND THE WORLD

1642
Tasmania is discovered by Dutch mariner Abel Tasman, who names the region after the governor of the Dutch East Indies, Anton Van Diemen.

1662
In England, King Charles II inaugurates the Royal Society for the pursuit and advance of the physical sciences.

1670
King Charles II grants the Hudson's Bay Company (HBC) all lands draining into Hudson Bay for the purpose of trading in furs.

1682
In North America, French explorer Rene-Robert La Salle claims the vast area drained by the Mississippi River (Louisiana) for France.

1684
HBC builds York Factory on the western shore of Hudson Bay.

1741
Russian explorer Vitus Bering establishes Russia's claim to northwestern North America.

1758-1762
Following French defeats during the Seven Years' War, England deports French settlers from Acadia (present-day Nova Scotia

Franklin and His Times	**Canada and the World**
	and New Brunswick) to England, France, and Louisiana.
	1763 The Treaty of Paris that ends the Seven Years' War cedes Louisiana to Spain.
	1768 Captain James Cook and Joseph Banks of the Royal Society lead a British scientific expedition to the southern Pacific Ocean.
	1770 Britain annexes the eastern seaboard of Australia and names it New South Wales.
	1771 Canadian explorer and fur trader Samuel Hearne reaches the Coppermine River.
1774 Thomas Adam Franklin (Franklin's oldest brother) is born.	**1774** Hearne selects the site for Cumberland House, the first inland fort of the HBC.
	1775 In North America, the American War of Independence begins.
	1776 The thirteen American colonies declare independence from Britain on July 4.
	1778 English explorer Captain James Cook sails into Bering Strait in

Franklin and His Times | **Canada and the World**

search of the western approach to the Northwest Passage; a wall of ice stops him.

1780
Willingham Franklin, Jr. (Franklin's second eldest brother) is born.

1780
Highland Scots, Canadien woodsmen, and Montreal businessmen and explorers join together in the North West Company (NWC) to trade in furs and resist the inland advances of the HBC.

Thomas Drummond, future botanist, is born in Scotland.

Elizabeth Fry, future prison reformer, is born in England.

1783
James Franklin (Franklin's third eldest brother) is born.

1783
The Treaty of Paris formally recognizes the United States of America (U.S.); colonists loyal to the British Crown (Loyalists) leave the U.S. and move into the British colonies to the north.

1784
George Arthur, future colonial governor, is born at Plymouth, England.

1786
John Franklin is born on April 16 at Spilsby, Lincolnshire, England, to Willingham and Hanah Weekes Franklin; John is the ninth of twelve children; eleven will survive infancy.

1786
Because the settlement of British convicts in the U.S. is no longer possible, a plan for their transport to New South Wales is adopted.

1787
The first fleet carrying convicts to Australia leaves Britain in May.

Franklin and His Times	**Canada and the World**
	John Richardson, future surgeon and naturalist, is born at Dumfries, Scotland.
	1788 The convict fleet arrives in Botany Bay; a better harbour is soon discovered to the north where Port Jackson (later Sydney) is established.
	1789 In France, the fall of the Bastille marks the symbolic beginning of the French Revolution.
	Scottish-born Canadian explorer Alexander Mackenzie reaches the Arctic Ocean overland from Lake Athabasca, affirming Hearne's finding that it was possible to traverse the Canadian Arctic over land.
	1791 The Constitution Act divides the old Province of Quebec into Lower and Upper Canada along the present-day Quebec-Ontario border.
	The Spanish explorer Galiano maps much of Canada's west coast; English explorer Captain George Vancouver spends the first of three summers as leader of a maritime expedition to explore the west coast of North America from California to Alaska.

Franklin and His Times / Canada and the World

1792
Franklin and His Times: Matthew Flinders, Franklin's uncle, sails with William Bligh, of the mutiny on the *Bounty* fame, on his second voyage.

1796
Franklin and His Times: Franklin first attends Louth Grammar School

1797
Franklin and His Times: Franklin travels with school friends to the village of Saltfleet, where he sees the sea for the first time.

Canada and the World: At the Battle of Tenerife, British admiral Horatio Nelson, having already lost the sight in his right eye in Corsica, loses his right arm.

1798
Canada and the World: George Vancouver publishes his journals, in which he claims to have proven the existence of the Northwest Passage.

Canada and the World: Englishmen George Bass and Matthew Flinders circumnavigate Van Diemen's Land.

1799
Franklin and His Times: Franklin tells his parents he wants to become a sailor; in order to discourage him, his father arranges for him to sail from Hull to Lisbon, a route that traverses the notorious Bay of Biscay.

Franklin and His Times: Eleanor Ann Porden, Franklin's future wife, is born.

Canada and the World: In France, Napoleon Bonaparte becomes First Consul.

Canada and the World: Britain and Russia invade the Netherlands in the hope that the Dutch will rise up against their French conquerors; the invasion is unsuccessful.

1800
Franklin and His Times: Franklin joins HMS *Polyphemus* as a first-class volunteer on March 9,

Canada and the World: Louisiana is returned to France in a secret treaty.

Franklin and His Times	**Canada and the World**
a month before his fourteenth birthday.	
1801 Franklin gets his first taste of battle on board the *Polyphemus* in the Battle of Copenhagen. In July, midshipman Franklin sails in HMS *Investigator* under his uncle, Captain Matthew Flinders, who plans to map the Australian coast.	**1801** The British navy under Horatio Nelson destroys the Danish navy in the Battle of Copenhagen; William Bligh is among the officers taking part.
1802 *Investigator* is beached for repairs on the coast of Australia; carpenters discover rotten timbers; during the voyage back to Port Jackson the ship leaks badly and is in danger of breaking up.	**1802** France concludes a peace treaty with Britain; Napoleon is made consul for life.
1803 *Investigator* is deemed unfit; on August 10, Flinders leaves on the *Porpoise* for England to find another ship; Franklin is with him; the *Porpoise* runs aground on an unmapped coral reef in Torres Strait between Australia and New Guinea; ninety-four men are shipwrecked on a sandbar with little hope of rescue; when rescue comes, Franklin goes to China; Flinders continues mapping; he is captured by the French at Mauritius and held captive for six years.	**1803** War between France and Britain is rekindled; Nelson is named Commander-in-Chief, Mediterranean; he patrols the south coast of France on HMS *Victory*; Napoleon prepares to invade England. France sells Louisiana to the U.S. Britain establishes Hobart Town in Van Diemen's Land; three-quarters of the first settlers are convicts.

Franklin and His Times

1804
Franklin returns to England from China as signal midshipman in a convoy of merchant ships; the commander outsmarts a squadron of French warships.

Franklin spends six weeks with his family in Lincolnshire; in August, he joins HMS *Bellerophon*; the ship spends a year blockading the French fleet at Brest.

1805
Bellerophon returns to England in the summer and then resumes blockade work at Cadiz and Cartagena.

Franklin is the signals officer on the *Bellerophon* at the Battle of Trafalgar; he interprets Nelson's famous order, "England expects that every man will do his duty," for his shipmates; it is his responsibility to make sure the flag is flying; Franklin is one of the few on the ship uninjured, although he loses some of his hearing from the noise of battle; he is singled out for displaying "very conspicuous zeal and ability."

1806
Franklin begins six years of blockading work.

Canada and the World

1804
In the presence of Pope Pious VII, Napoleon crowns himself Emperor of the French.

1805
Nelson chases the French and Spanish fleets across the Atlantic and back.

In October, during the Battle of Trafalgar, twenty-seven British ships meet the combined French and Spanish fleets near the Strait of Gibraltar for the last great naval engagement fought under sail; Nelson is mortally wounded during the battle; his body is returned to England preserved in a cask of rum.

1806
Having defeated Austria, Prussia, and Russia, Napoleon controls most of Europe; although he imposes a continental blockade against Britain, the British still control the seas; this enrages the U.S., which is looking for an

Franklin and His Times | **Canada and the World**

excuse to invade Upper and Lower Canada.

1807
Franklin transfers to the HMS *Bedford* as master's mate; he is soon promoted to acting lieutenant.

Thomas Franklin commits suicide after his financial speculation ends disastrously.

1808
In February, Lieutenant John Franklin sails with the fleet to escort the deposed Portuguese royal family to Brazil; without family money to enhance his income, Franklin is miserable is Brazil, which is dirty, unhealthy and overcrowded.

1808
While looking for the mouth of the Columbia River, explorer Simon Fraser discovers the river that will be named after him.

1810
Franklin returns to England in August; his mother dies in November.

Captain Matthew Flinders is released from captivity in Mauritius.

1810
American troops take control of Baton Rouge from the Spanish.

1811
Major-General Isaac Brock becomes commander of British forces in Upper Canada and provisional administrator of the government.

1812
Impatient with blockade work, Franklin applies for a transfer, but his request is denied.

1812
The U.S. Congress declares war against Britain on June 18 and

Franklin and His Times

Canada and the World

attacks Canada; Isaac Brock is killed at Queenston Heights.

Future English novelist Charles Dickens is born.

1813
British forces defeat Napoleon in Spain.

Neither British nor American forces are able to control Lake Ontario; depleted American forces leave Upper Canada.

1814
In the second of two years spent escorting merchant convoys to the West Indies, the *Bedford*, with Franklin on board, is ordered to sail to New Orleans, where the British fleet is gathering to attack the Americans.

Matthew Flinders dies, never having regained his health lost when he was a captive.

1814
A series of battles exhausts both sides in the war; the British burn Washington, D.C. in August; both sides capture and lose territory; the war ends with the signing of the Treaty of Ghent on December 14; all captured territory is returned.

Allied forces of Europe defeat Napoleon and send him into exile on the island of Elba near Corsica.

1815
News of the end of the war has not reached the combatants at New Orleans; the British navy attacks U.S. gunboats on Lake Borgne; Franklin is wounded but is not out of action for long; he is mentioned in dispatches and receives a medal for his role in the attack; the *Bedford* returns to Britain in May.

1815
At the Battle of New Orleans, two thousand British soldiers are killed or wounded.

Napoleon returns from exile and rules for one hundred days; in June, forces under the Duke of Wellington defeat him at Waterloo; the end of the Napoleonic Wars puts many sailors and ships out of work.

FRANKLIN AND HIS TIMES

1818
Having been on half-pay since 1815, Lieutenant Franklin welcomes the opportunity to be second-in-command of the British Polar expedition; he takes command of the *Trent*, a small whaler; among the visitors to the ships as they prepare to sail is Eleanor Ann Porden, a young woman with an interest in science and poetry.

The expedition sails on April 25; the boats leak, heavy ice blocks their way, walrus attack the longboats, icebergs calf, the boats become icebound; the expedition is finally compelled to turn for home; Franklin gets his first taste of Arctic conditions; attention now focuses exclusively on finding the Northwest Passage.

Franklin accepts the leadership of an expedition to map the Arctic coast of Canada east from the Coppermine River, to study the natural history, examine the aurora borealis, and to take detailed

CANADA AND THE WORLD

1817
Whaling Master William Scoresby returns from Baffin Bay in the Canadian Arctic with the news that normally icebound parts of the Greenland coast are ice free.

English naval officer and explorer John Ross commands an expedition to explore Baffin Bay.

1818
In England, the government mounts two Arctic expeditions: one is to sail through the Northwest Passage from the Atlantic to the Pacific and the other to sail straight north, discover the North Pole, continue through the Bering Strait and on to the Sandwich Islands (Hawaii); the expeditions mark the opening of the golden age of British Arctic exploration.

Edward Parry is given command of the expedition charged with sailing through the Northwest Passage.

A treaty between Britain and the U.S. sets the northern boundaries of the Louisiana Purchase along the forty-ninth parallel.

Mary Wollstonecraft Shelley's novel *Frankenstein* is published.

Franklin and His Times | **Canada and the World**

readings of all aspects of magnetic force.

1819

On May 28, the three ships of Franklin's first expedition set sail, almost leaving midshipman George Back behind; they reach the entrance to Hudson Bay on August 7, meet Inuit for the first time on August 8, and arrive at York Factory on August 30.

On September 9, Franklin and a party of four, including naturalist Dr. John Richardson and midshipman Back, leave York Factory with the support of HBC and NWC voyageurs and Aboriginal People; they go inland by riverboat, across Lake Winnipeg, and up the Saskatchewan River to reach Cumberland House on October 23.

1819

Danish physicist Hans C. Oersted discovers electromagnetism.

Parry sails for the Canadian Arctic on May 9; he explores Prince Regent Inlet and reaches farther west along the south shore of Melville Island than anyone has before; his will be the first modern expedition to winter in the High Arctic.

A treaty between Spain and the U.S. sets the western boundaries of the Louisiana Purchase.

1820

In mid-January, Franklin and a small party, including George Back, leave Cumberland House for Fort Chipewyan, an NWC outpost on Lake Athabasca; the party travels almost all the way on snowshoes, which they find difficult to master; they arrive on March 26.

Reluctant voyageurs, a scarcity of food, and the hostility between the NWC and the HBC make preparation difficult, but Franklin presses on, this time by canoe; he arrives at Fort Providence on Great Slave Lake, the most north-

1820

Edward Parry returns from a successful voyage to the Canadian Arctic.

Explorer Sir Alexander Mackenzie dies in Britain.

FRANKLIN AND HIS TIMES

erly trading outpost, on July 28; the Copper (Yellowknife) First Nation agrees to assist him; the party arrives at the wintering site on August 20, names it Fort Enterprise and builds two log houses in preparation for winter.

1821
In January, Franklin is promoted to Commander; in June, he and a party of nineteen travel down the Coppermine River retracing Hearne's route to the Arctic coast in July.

Unlike Hearne, Franklin and his party, which includes Richardson and Back, continue east along the coast. They are determined to map over one thousand kilometers between the Coppermine River and Hudson Bay, but the convoluted shoreline and a shortage of food leads Franklin to order a return to Fort Enterprise across the barren lands; winter sets in early; when they reach Fort Enterprise on October 11 they find it deserted; by the time relief arrives on November 7, eleven members of the party are dead.

1822
Having slowly regained their health, Franklin and his men sail for England in the spring; Franklin arrives in London in October to find himself a hero; he is promoted to captain and becomes a member of the Royal Society.

CANADA AND THE WORLD

1821
English physicist and chemist Michael Faraday demonstrates electromagnetic rotation.

The HBC absorbs the NWC.

Napoleon dies on St. Helena.

Edward Parry leaves England again for the Canadian Arctic.

Franklin and His Times

Franklin's book, *Narrative of a Journey to the Shores of the Polar Sea in the Years 1819, 20, 21, and 22* sells briskly; its success reinforces his mistaken idea that using aboriginals and voyageurs was a mistake.

1823
Franklin's father dies; Franklin spends time at the family home at Spilsby, Lincolnshire.

On August 19, Franklin marries Eleanor Ann Porden; she is the author of a well-received book of poetry; she has TB.

1824
Franklin's daughter, Eleanor, is born in June; her mother's condition deteriorates rapidly, but despite this and with his wife's blessing, Franklin prepares for his second expedition.

Sir Willingham Franklin, Jr., a Supreme Court judge in Madras, dies of cholera.

1825
On February 16, Franklin leaves England on his second expedition, accompanied again by Richardson and Back; on the shores of Lake Huron he receives the news that his wife died six days after his departure from England.

Carefully planned and with supplies and equipment sent on ahead, Franklin's second expedi-

Canada and the World

1823
Edward Parry returns to England having discovered Fury and Hecla Strait and confirmed Lancaster Sound as the entrance to the Northwest Passage; he proposes a third attempt to explore the Passage.

1824
Parry sails to the Canadian Arctic to explore Prince Regent Inlet; while wintering there, one of his two ships, *Fury*, is damaged and abandoned; her supplies are cached on Fury Beach.

1825
Parry returns to England.

Van Diemen's Land becomes a separate colony from New South Wales.

Robert Dunsmuir, future coal magnate on Vancouver Island, is born in Scotland.

Franklin and His Times

tion is going well; he reaches the Mackenzie River on August 2 well ahead of schedule, unfurls the flag that Eleanor has given him, and loses no time returning to his winter quarters at Fort Franklin.

1826
In early July, two parties set out from the mouth of the Mackenzie River - Richardson's party goes east and Franklin's (with Back) goes west; Franklin's group is swarmed by aggressive Inuit who take all the trade goods; Franklin names the site Pillage Point; on July 27, the party crosses into Russian territory; having mapped 981 kilometres of unexplored coast, they turn back on August 17, encountering storms and friendlier Inuit and arriving back at Fort Franklin in September; both expedition parties have had successful summers.

1827
Franklin, with five sailors and two guides, leaves Fort Franklin in February and reaches Cumberland House in June; the expedition has collected hundreds of samples and much scientific data; they meet Richardson, who has travelled west to meet botanist Thomas Drummond. Drummond has spent two years collecting specimens on the prairies.

Franklin and Richardson take a leisurely journey home, visiting

Canada and the World

1827
Wellington is made commander-in-chief of the British army.

The Parry expedition reaches 82 degrees 45 minutes north, the closest anyone will get to the North Pole for fifty years; Parry's second-in-command is James Clark Ross, an authority on magnetism and a good naturalist and taxidermist.

Franklin and His Times

Montreal and New York and arriving in Liverpool on September 26.

Franklin is showered with recognition: a gold medal from the French Geographical Society, a knighthood, and an honorary degree from Oxford.

1828
Franklin courts Jane Griffin, a woman he has met through his first wife; during the summer, they travel to Russia; Franklin meets Alexander, the ten-year-old czarevich (heir to the throne).

On November 5, Franklin marries Jane and they honeymoon in Paris, where he is a celebrity.

1830
Having spent two years of "vanity, trifling and idleness," Franklin is relieved to be given command of the frigate HMS *Rainbow*; in November he sails for the Mediterranean.

Canada and the World

Sanford Fleming, future Canadian railway surveyor, is born in Scotland.

1828
Wellington becomes Prime Minister of Britain.

Thomas Drummond becomes curator of the botanical garden in Belfast.

1829
John Ross commands a privately funded Arctic expedition into Lancaster Sound accompanied by his nephew, James Clark Ross.

The Peace of Adrianople ends the Russo-Turkish War; Turkey acknowledges Greece's independence.

1830
James Clark Ross reaches Victory Point on King William Island.

John Irving, future lieutenant on the last Franklin expedition, wins a medal for mathematical achievement from the Royal Naval College, Portsmouth, England.

Franklin and His Times

Canada and the World

George IV, King of England, dies and is succeeded by his brother, William.

1831
On June 1, James Clark Ross discovers the North Magnetic Pole.

1832
Having cruised the Mediterranean for two years with stops at Malta, Nauplia, and Corfu, where Lady Jane Franklin visits him, Franklin sails to Patras in southern Greece; in Patras he intervenes in a local dispute between British merchants and the governor using a conciliatory tone and the presence of his twenty-six-gun frigate.

One week later, Franklin's diplomatic intervention in another crisis allows Patras to experience an unusually quiet Easter.

1833
In February the new king of Greece arrives and the *Rainbow* goes home; Franklin is commended for his "calm and steady conduct" and his "judgment and forbearance."

1833
His ship, *Victory*, having been icebound in the Canadian Arctic for four winters, John Ross and his nephew, James Clark Ross, are finally able to return to England, where John is knighted.

1834
On January 8, Franklin leaves the *Rainbow*; although King William interviews him, the First Lord of the Admiralty brushes Franklin off when he asks for a new posting.

1834
George Back is chosen over more experienced candidates to lead another Northwest Passage expedition aboard HMS *Terror*.

Franklin and His Times | **Canada and the World**

James Franklin, soldier, surveyor, mapmaker, dies.

1835
Botanist Thomas Drummond dies in Havana, Cuba.

1836
Franklin applies to the Colonial Office for a position; he becomes governor of Van Diemen's Land; he sails for the south Pacific.

1837
Franklin and his family arrive in Van Diemen's Land; he finds that his predecessor, George Arthur, has created a totalitarian state with a brutal system of dealing with convicts; Franklin is dependent on Arthur's associates to run the colony smoothly; settlers soon develop a strong dislike for Franklin and for his wife, Jane, who is seen to be interfering.

Jane forms the "Tasmanian Ladies' Society for the Reformation of Female Prisoners," but it is unwelcome and short-lived; she has more success encouraging the arts and natural history; she is the first woman to travel overland from Melbourne to Sydney.

1837
Rebellions in Upper and Lower Canada

The first episode of *Oliver Twist*, by Charles Dickens, is published.

Victoria becomes Queen of Great Britain and the Empire.

1838
George Arthur, former governor of Van Diemen's Land, becomes lieutenant-governor of Upper Canada.

Franklin and His Times

1840
Economic development in Van Diemen's Land reaches a peak, to be followed by a severe depression.

In August, the *Erebus* and *Terror* arrive at Hobart; Franklin meets James Clark Ross and Francis Crozier; he supplies convict labour to build a magnetic observatory for Ross outside Hobart; Ross throws a dress ball in his honour aboard the *Erebus*.

1841
Franklin goes out to meet Ross's ships when they return from Antarctica;

Canada and the World

1839
James Clark Ross sails from London with orders to explore and circumnavigate the Antarctic continent; he commands HMS *Erebus* and his second-in-command, Francis Rawdon Moira Crozier, commands HMS *Terror*.

Louis Jacques Mande Daguerre, a French painter and physicist, announces the invention of the daguerreotype, an early photographic process.

In the aftermath of the rebellions in Upper and Lower Canada, 29 men are hanged and 141 are deported to Australia.

1841
George Arthur is knighted for his role in uniting Upper and Lower Canada; he returns to England and becomes the Governor of Bombay the following year.

Franklin and His Times

Franklin's niece and Jane's companion, Sophia Cracroft, falls in love with James Clark Ross, but he remains faithful to his fiancée; Crozier falls in love with Sophia, but she turns down his proposal of marriage.

1842
In March, Franklin and Jane and a small party struggle through the rain-soaked wilderness between Hobart and Macquarie Harbour, where they rendezvous with a ship just as it has given up on them; starvation threatens when storms delay the ship's departure.

1844
Having been discredited by John Montagu, his colonial secretary, Franklin is recalled to England unjustly deemed to have failed in colonial politics.

1845
Franklin, though almost fifty-nine years old, is offered leadership of the latest Arctic expedition; his second-in-command is Francis Crozier; his well-equipped ships are *Erebus* and *Terror*; his mission is to complete the Northwest Passage and conduct scientific investigation.

In May, a daguerreotype preserves the moment before departure in the Great Cabin of the *Erebus*; Franklin has the flu and has recently had a premonition about his own death; the expedition

Canada and the World

1845
James Clark Ross agrees to stay at home when his wife asks him not to undertake any more long voyages.

Franklin and His Times

leaves amid high expectations for its success; Franklin is in high spirits; in July, from Greenland, he writes to his friends in England to ask them to "comfort and assist" Jane; ice stops his first two attempts to find the Passage; he circumnavigates Cornwallis Island and settles in for the winter beside Beechey Island.

1846
During the winter, three of Franklin's men die of TB-related illnesses; in summer, the expedition works its way down to a position north of King William Island; on September 12, Franklin is beset in the Beaufort Ice Stream; he docks his ships for winter in a stable ice floe.

1847
Franklin sends out a sledging expedition to examine the west coast of King William Island and complete the Northwest Passage under Lieutenant Graham Gore, who leaves brief optimistic notes in cairns to mark his progress.

On June 11, Franklin dies unexpectedly at the age of sixty-one; Crozier assumes command; the ice does not break up and the expedition faces another winter; men die of scurvy and lead poisoning from poorly soldered canned food.

Canada and the World

1847
In reaction to British government designs to make Van Diemen's Land "the jail of the Empire," a movement against the transportation of convicts is launched.

Franklin and His Times

1848
In the spring, Crozier orders the 105 survivors to head south overland in search of fresh food; they retrieve one of the messages left in a cairn and add their change of plans to the message; some men die in their tracks; some die at a large camp on the south shore of King William Island; some die beneath an upturned boat at Starvation Cove on the Canadian mainland and some beside a boat on the way back to the ships; a few make it back to the ships but scurvy, starvation, and ice prevent them from escaping the Arctic.

In England, nothing has been heard from the Franklin expedition for three years; a three-way search is organized: Sir James Clark Ross approaches through Lancaster Sound, Captain Henry Kellet comes from Bering Strait, and John Rae and Sir John Richardson trek overland from the Mackenzie River. No one finds any definite traces of the expedition.

Canada and the World

1848
Britain's Royal Navy begins to change from sail to steam power.

Revolutions erupt in several European countries.

1849
George Mercer Dawson (future Canadian geologist, explorer, and mapmaker) is born in Pictou, Nova Scotia.

Franklin and His Times

1850
More search parties set out: Richard Collinson and Robert McClure search from the west,

Canada and the World

1850
The first episode of *Bleak House*, by Charles Dickens, is published.

Franklin and His Times

Horatio Austin and William Penny from the east; the HBC sends Sir John Ross; E.J. De Haven heads an American expedition; Lady Franklin finances an expedition under Charles Forsyth.

Franklin's first wintering site is discovered at Beechey Island but gives no clues as to his fate.

1851
Lady Franklin sends out another search expedition.

1852
The British Admiralty sends out its last and greatest expedition under Sir Edward Belcher. This expedition also looks for McClure and Collinson, who have not been heard from.

1854
Sir Edward Belcher returns from his search for Franklin having rescued McClure, who, with his crew, is awarded the Admiralty prize for completing the Northwest Passage.

John Rae of the HBC wins 10,000 pounds for settling Franklin's fate when he returns to England with some relics obtained from the Inuit and stories told by the Inuit of abandoned boats, starving men, and cannibalism; the Royal Navy

Canada and the World

1853
Transportation of convicts officially ends.

1854
Britain, France, and Turkey declare war on Russia in the Crimea; Lord Tennyson publishes the poem "The Charge of the Light Brigade."

Franklin and His Times

declares Franklin and all his men dead and stops their double pay; public figures like Charles Dickens denounce Rae.

1859
Leading an expedition financed by Lady Jane Franklin, Francis Leopold McClintock discovers clothing, supplies, and a note at Victory Point on King William Island; farther along the coast the men find an abandoned ship's boat and the scattered bones of Franklin's men.

Canada and the World

1855
Czar Alexander II ascends the throne of Russia.

Van Diemen's Land officially becomes Tasmania.

1857
Ottawa is chosen capital of Canada.

1859
Charles Darwin publishes *On the Origin of the Species by Means of Natural Selection*.

1861
Emily Pauline Johnson, future Canadian aboriginal poet, is born near Brantford, Ontario.

The American Civil War begins.

1865
Sir John Richardson dies at "Lancrigg," England.

American President Lincoln is assassinated; the American Civil War ends.

Franklin and His Times | **Canada and the World**

1867
Canadian Confederation unites Ontario, Quebec, Nova Scotia, and New Brunswick.

1869
American explorer Charles Francis Hall searches the southeast region of King William Island for the Franklin party.

1869
Louis Riel leads the Red River Rebellion.

Robert Dunsmuir discovers the Wellington coal seam on Vancouver Island.

1870
Manitoba joins Canadian Confederation.

1871
British Columbia joins Canadian Confederation.

Emily Carr, future Canadian painter, is born in Victoria, B.C.

1875
Jane Franklin dies; weeks later, George Back unveils a marble monument to Franklin in Westminster Abbey.

1876
Trucanini, the last Tasmanian Aborigine, dies; her death marks the end of the only case of true genocide in British history.

1879
American Lieutenant Frederick Schwatka makes the first summer search of King William Island. He finds the skeleton of Lieutenant

Franklin and His Times

John Irving at Victory Point in a shallow grave with his medal for mathematical achievement lying beside the skull. Searches continue into the 20th century. Thirty-two in all, they expand the knowledge of the Canadian Arctic immensely; many more discoveries and new scientific techniques lead in the direction of solving the mystery of what happened to Franklin and his party.

Canada and the World

1881
Czar Alexander II is assassinated.

1882
Robert Koch discovers the tubercle bacillus and demonstrates its role in causing TB.

Acknowledgments

The quotations in the text are either taken from original documents in Polar Archives or from material quoted in the referenced publications. I use these sources with thanks to the authors or editors. The staff at the Scott Polar Research Institute in Cambridge; at the National Maritime Museum in Greenwich; and at the Royal Geographical Society in London, England were extremely helpful with the research upon which this and my other Franklin-related books are based.

An excellent source for up-to-date information on the ever-continuing struggle to solve the mystery of Franklin's third expedition as well as book reviews and links to related sites, can be found at http://www.ric.edu/rpotter/index.html

My thanks to everyone who has struggled along a bleak Arctic shore searching for a fragment of cloth or a bone which might add another piece to the puzzle.

Sources Consulted

BEATTIE, Owen and GEIGER, John. *Frozen in Time: Unlocking the Secrets of the Franklin Expedition.* Vancouver: Douglas & McIntyre, 1992.

CYRIAX, Richard. *Sir John Franklin's Last Arctic Expedition.* Plaistow & Sutton Coldfield, The Arctic Press, 1997.

DAVIS, Richard (ed.). *Sir John Franklin's Journals and Correspondence: The First Arctic Land Expedition, 1819-1822.* Toronto: The Champlain Society, 1995.

DAVIS, Richard (ed.). *Sir John Franklin's Journals and Correspondence: The Second Arctic Land Expedition, 1825-1827.* Toronto: The Champlain Society, 1998.

FRANKLIN, John. *Narrative of a Journey to the Shores of the Polar Sea in the Years 1819, 20, 21, and 22.* Edmonton: Hurtig, 1969.

HOUSTON, Stuart (ed.). *To the Arctic by Canoe 1819-1821: The Journal and Paintings of Robert Hood, Midshipman with Franklin.* Montreal and Kingston: McGill-Queen's University Press, 1974.

HOUSTON, Stuart (ed.). *Arctic Ordeal: The Journal of John Richardson, Surgeon-Naturalist with*

Franklin, 1820-1822. Montreal and Kingston: McGill-Queen's University Press, 1984.

HOUSTON, Stuart (ed.). *Arctic Artist: The Journal and Paintings of George Back, Midshipman with Franklin, 1819-1822*. Montreal and Kingston: McGill-Queen's University Press, 1994.

HUGHES, Robert. *The Fatal Shore: The Epic of Australia's Founding*. New York: Vintage Books, 1988.

KEEGAN, John. *The Price of Admiralty: The Evolution of Naval Warfare*. New York: Viking, 1989.

LAMB, G. F. *Franklin Happy Voyager: Being the Life and Death of Sir John Franklin*. London: Ernest Benn, 1956.

LAMBERT, R. S. *Franklin of the Arctic: A Life of Adventure*. Toronto: McClelland & Stewart, 1949.

MCCLINTOCK, Francis L. *A Narrative of the Discovery of the Fate of Sir John Franklin and his Companions*. Edmonton: Hurtig, 1972.

MORDAL, Jacques, *25 Centuries of Sea Warfare*. London: Futura, 1976.

NANTON, Paul. *Arctic Breakthrough: Franklin's Expeditions, 1819-1847*. Toronto: Clarke, Irwin & Company, 1970.

ROSS, M. J. *Polar Pioneers John Ross and James Clark Ross*. Montreal and Kingston: McGill-Queen's University Press, 1994.

WOODMAN, David. *Unravelling the Franklin Mystery: Inuit Testimony*. Montreal and Kingston: McGill-Queen's University Press, 1992.

WOODMAN, David. *Strangers Among Us*. Montreal and Kingston: McGill- Queen's University Press, 1995.

Index